LOCOMOTION PAPERS

The Culm Valley Light Railway

Tiverton Junction to Hemyock

by
Colin G. Maggs

THE OAKWOOD PRESS

© Oakwood Press & Colin G. Maggs 2006

British Library Cataloguing in Publication Data
A Record for this book is available from the British Library
ISBN 0 85361 652 3
ISBN 978 085361 652 8

Typeset by Oakwood Graphics.
Repro by PKmediaworks, Cranborne, Dorset.
Printed by Cambrian Printers, Aberystwyth, Ceredigion.

All rights reserved. No part of this book may be reproduced or transmitted in any form or by any means, electronic or mechanical, including photocopying, recording or by any information storage and retrieval system, without permission from the Publisher in writing.

'14XX' class 0-4-2T No. 1440 leaving Tiverton Junction on 12th October, 1957 with the 1.40 pm to Hemyock. The coach is an ex-Barry Railway vehicle. *R.E. Toop*

Title page: No. 1420 shunting milk tanks after arrival with the 5.07 pm ex-Tiverton Junction, 15th July, 1960. Notice the fire buckets lined up in front of Hemyock East ground frame. *M.H. Walshaw*

Front cover: '14XX' class 0-4-2T No. 1421 at Hemyock with the 1.40 pm from Tiverton Junction with an ex-Eastern Region coach, 8th June, 1961. *Author*

Rear cover, top: 204 hp diesel-mechanical 0-6-0 shunter No. D2141 shunts its freight train at Hemyock, 31st August, 1965. The former large refreshment room can be seen above No. D2141. *Michael Farr*

Rear cover, bottom: '14XX' class 0-4-2T No. 1451 is ready to depart Hemyock with a train for Tiverton Junction, 22nd May, 1961. The dairy is in the background. *Michael Farr*

Published by The Oakwood Press (Usk), P.O. Box 13, Usk, Mon., NP15 1YS.
E-mail: sales@oakwoodpress.co.uk
Website: www.oakwoodpress.co.uk

Contents

	Introduction	5
Chapter One	Planning the Culm Valley Light Railway	7
Chapter Two	Construction	17
Chapter Three	Opening and the Early Years	23
Chapter Four	Consolidation and Growth	39
Chapter Five	Description of the Line	47
Chapter Six	Events Leading to Closure	83
Chapter Seven	Locomotives	103
Chapter Eight	Coaches and Other Rolling Stock	113
Chapter Nine	Passenger Train Services	119
Chapter Ten	Permanent Way and Signalling	131
Chapter Eleven	Mishaps	138
Appendix One	Bridges on the Culm Valley Branch	139
Appendix Two	Log of Journey: Tiverton Junction to Hemyock, 8th June, 1963	141
	Bibliography	142
	Acknowledgements	143
	Index	144

An 0-4-2T, three milk tanks and clerestory roof coach No. 2312 at Hemyock c.1949.
M.E.J. Deane courtesy Ian Bennett

204 hp diesel-mechanical 0-6-0 shunter No. D2141 at Tiverton Junction, 31st August, 1965 with a grain wagon for Uffculme. The signal box may be seen at the top right. *Michael Farr*

Introduction

In 1870 what did most Victorians know of the Culm Valley in Devon? . . . Nothing or very little. An exception was Arthur Pain whose brother lived at Hemyock. Pain was a proponent of light railways and had been trained by R.P. Brereton, I.K. Brunel's chief assistant.

Horse trams had become familiar in Britain's larger cities and Pain envisaged a scheme whereby the characteristics of a railway and tramway could be combined to produce a relatively cheap line in an area where a full-scale railway would not be an economic proposition.

Pain's plan was for a track with minimal earthworks and thus have a low cost of construction while instead of erecting stations, expenses could be kept down by simply picking up passengers where the line met roads at level crossings.

Where better than to try out his idea than in the Culm Valley which had industry, farming and the tourist potential of the Wellington Monument only three miles from Hemyock, the great exploits of the Duke still within living memory? The district had been depicted in R.D. Blackmore's lesser-known romantic novel *Perlycross* which told of a glamorous Spanish-born heroine.

Blackmore's father had been curate-in-charge of Culmstock. The settlements of Perlycombe, Perlycross and Perliton, featured in the novel, were respectively Hemyock, Culmstock and Uffculme. The book also describes the way of life for the greenstone miners who dug the product from horizontal adits in Blackborough and Poncydown on the boundary of Uffculme, Sheldon and Kentisbeare parishes. Greenstone was used for grinding, but the industry was killed by imported and much cheaper Carborundum, or silicon carbide, discovered by Edward G. Acheson in 1891. Until 1929 when boron carbide was invented, Carborundum was the hardest synthetic material known. Thus greenstone never became a major traffic on the Culm Valley Light Railway (CVLR).

The River Culm rises three miles over the county border on the Blackdown Hills in Somerset. It give its name to several settlements on its banks and, in the 19th century, powered corn and cloth mills. After passing through Cullompton, it makes a confluence with the River Exe just north of Exeter.

Two recent Acts of Parliament favoured Pain's proposal. The Railway Construction Facilities Act of 1864 permitted a railway to be built without the need for an Act, if all landowners on the route agreed to sell the land required by the railway company. This facility avoided the considerable legal expenses of obtaining an Act.

The Regulation of Railways Act, passed four years later in 1868, enabled a light railway to be constructed under conditions laid down by the Board of Trade. A 'light railway' - the term first appeared in the 1868 Act - was generally defined as a line allowing a maximum weight of 8 tons per axle and a speed limit of 25 mph. The estimated cost of the CVLR was £3,000 per mile, which was only about a quarter of the cost of a normal branch line. Pain envisaged that landowners would keenly support the scheme due to the increased value it would bring to their property and trade.

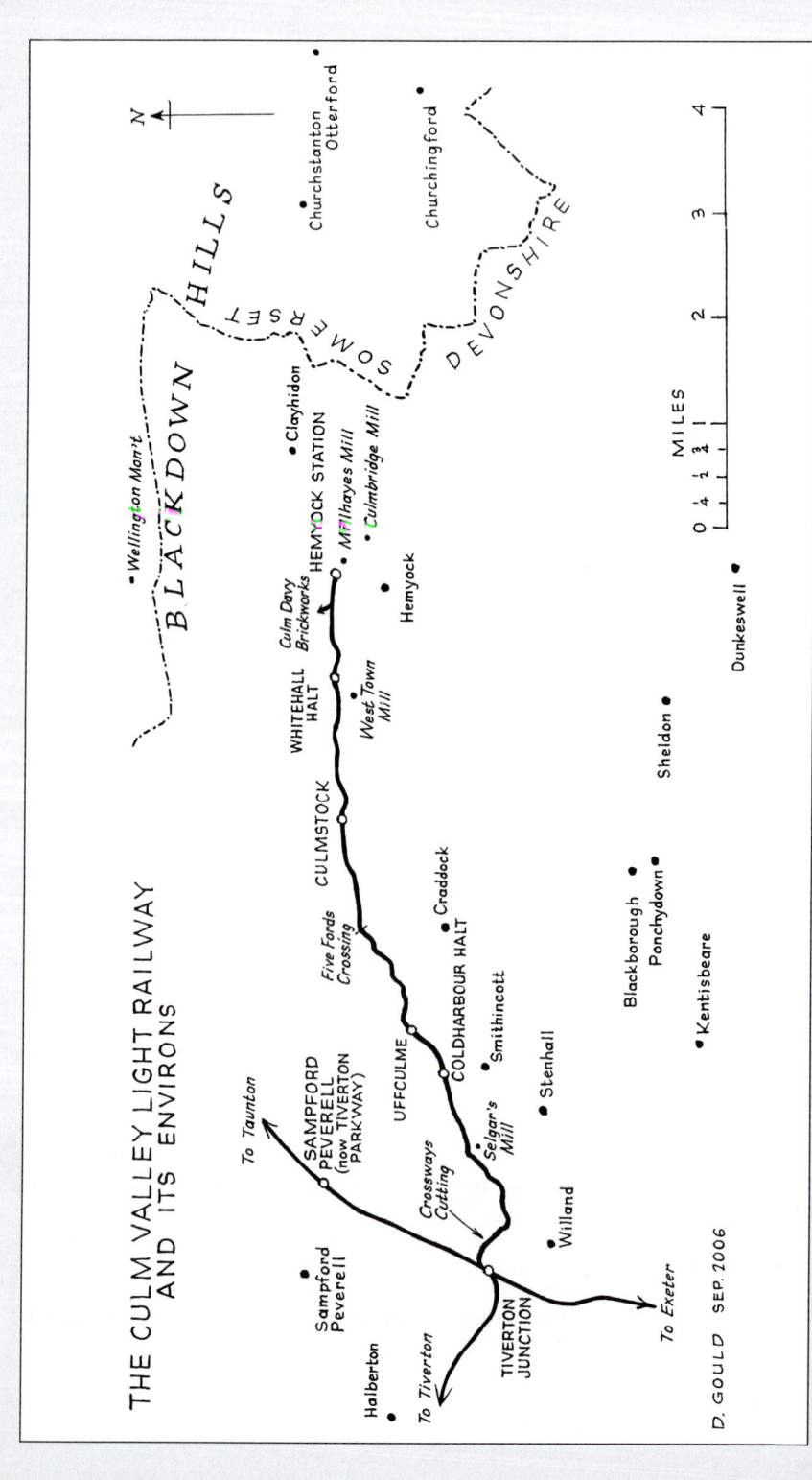

Chapter One

Planning the Culm Valley Light Railway

On 15th May, 1872 a large and influential meeting of landowners, farmers and traders was held at the George Inn, Uffculme. William Furze of the Uffculme Brewery took the chair and introduced Arthur Pain, who outlined the proposal of a railway from the Bristol & Exeter Railway (B&E) at Tiverton Junction to Hemyock, with sidings serving Selgar's Mills between Willand and Uffculme, and Messrs Fox's factory at Uffculme station. Uffculme station was to be situated in a field between the gas works and the river. A siding would serve for the joint use of Southey and Woodhayne farms. The line would then cross the River Culm to serve a mill and factory. One cottage required demolition, but this was the only building needing to be commandeered in the whole length of the line. A siding near Clements' bridge would cater for farms at Clements, West Town and the mill; likewise Whitehall siding would serve both farm and mill. Another siding would run to Millhayes Mill and after the main line crossed the river, a siding at Hemyock would serve another farm and mill.

To encourage landowners to support the scheme, the whole route was designed to avoid hedge severance as much as possible and so minimize the inconvenience of owning small parcels of land. Showing foresight, Pain proposed standard gauge, rather than the B&E's broad gauge.

The *Tiverton Gazette* of 21st May, 1872 reported:

What they intended to construct was a thoroughly cheap, or what was termed a light line . . . one that followed as much as possible the surface of the ground; that crossed roads on the level . . . The permanent way was of a lighter design than on the main line - he believed they saved 50 per cent in this respect - and the stations would only consist of a platform and shed.

Pain said that a similar light railway constructed by the Duke of Buckingham was returning a profit of 13 per cent. (This was the Wotton Tramway built from Quainton Road station on the Aylesbury & Buckingham Railway to Brill, principally to serve the Duke's estate. The cost of this 6½ mile-long line, including sidings and two goods shed, was less then £1,400 a mile, but as the Duke owned the land, there was no charge for this.)

The plan of building the CVLR under the Railway Construction Facilities Act was scotched when William Farrant observed that he knew one landowner who would not offer his land willingly and would require the compulsion of an Act of Parliament. Pain responded by claiming that landowners would not object if offered fair terms. The meeting closed with a pledge to support the line and a committee was appointed to arrange other public meetings throughout the district. The editorial column in the *Tiverton Gazette* commented: 'We heartily wish the promoters success'.

The first meeting of the committee, set up on 15th May, met at the Ilminster Inn, Uffculme on 19th June, 1872. Pain said that he had prepared plans and a draft Prospectus. He estimated the cost of the line at £3,000 a mile which compared very favourably with other single track branch lines, such as the Cheddar Valley at £12,000 per mile and Norton Fitzwarren to Watchet at almost £13,000. Frederick Pollard was appointed Secretary of the CVLR at a salary of £50 per annum. It was revealed that the only landowners opposing the scheme were the Misses Wood and George Coombes who owned Selgar's Mill.

The meeting at the New Inn, Hemyock on 5th August was chaired by Edward Lutley, farmer and landowner at Whitehall. He proposed that the line should terminate at Millhayes Mill, north of Hemyock, rather than at Culmbridge Mill to the east of Hemyock. He reasoned that, should the line ever be extended to join the London & South Western Railway's (LSWR) Salisbury to Exeter line, this would then form the most convenient site of Hemyock station, whereas Culmbridge was not on the best route to the LSWR. Others pointed out that Culmbridge was at the convergence of roads from Clayhidon, Churchstanton, Otterford, Upottery, Luppitt and Dukeswell and so a station at Culmbridge would serve 3,000 more people. (In the event, Hemyock station was sited at Millhayes.)

A meeting of the committee of promoters and shareholders of the proposed CVLR was held in the Commercial Inn, Uffculme on 18th November. It was announced that terms had been arranged with 30 of the principal landowners, but two had objected, so the committee had to apply for an Act of Parliament in order to compel them to sell their land. Ironically on the evening of 16th November, the CVLR's solicitors in London received a letter from the two objectors saying that they had abandoned their opposition and would sell their land. Unfortunately because by this date the Directors had given notice to go to Parliament, the Directors were obliged to do so.

One advantage of the withdrawal of the opposition was that construction could start before the Act was obtained, but events showed that this opportunity was not seized. The meeting elected the company's first Directors:

Henry Samuel Ellis	Exeter	(A Director of the Bristol & Exeter Railway)
Charles John Follett	Exeter	(Mayor of Exeter and a solicitor)
William Furze	Uffculme	
Edward Lutley	Hemyock	
Henry Aylmer Porter	Exeter	
Henry Drew Thomas	Exeter	

These Directors relieved the provisional committee of its responsibilities. The company's bankers were the Tiverton & Devonshire Bank and the auditors William Cotton, manager of the National Provincial Bank, Exeter, and John Cave New, local landowner.

The meeting:

> Resolved unanimously that in the opinion of this meeting the proposed light railway through the Culm Valley to Hemyock is a sound and substantial undertaking both locally and financially and one especially deserving the support of the agricultural and trading interests in the district and of the public generally and that this meeting pledges itself to advance the prosperity of the line by every means in its power.

Pain was to be paid 5 per cent of the estimated cost of £22,500, but receive this remuneration in shares and not cash.

A statement of traffic sent to Tiverton Junction by the various mill and factory owners in the Culm Valley was submitted to J.C. Wall, the B&E's General Manager, resulting in him agreeing to enter into working arrangements as soon as the CVLR was completed. The B&E looked favourably on the scheme, but required certain conditions such as proper passenger and goods stations and that the road bridges at Willand, carrying the road to Halberton and what is now the B3181, should be constructed of stone or brick, not timber. The B&E accepted the light-weight rails, but insisted on better quality sleepers and ballast with a depth of not less than 15 inches.

The B&E undertook to work the line for 50 per cent of the gross receipts and allow a rebate of five per cent on traffic passing to and from its line. It also guaranteed the interest of debentures and contributed £105 towards the preliminary expense of promoting the Culm Valley Bill in Parliament and would allow its General Manager and Engineer to give evidence in support of the Bill.

The *Tiverton Gazette* of 26th November, 1872 reported Pain's comments:

> I might safely say that if people living in the locality do not look sharp, they will get no shares at all. The capital is small and there are many gentlemen of influence around willing to take shares . . . I know of no line which has been received with so much public approval.

Unfortunately for the investors, this statement proved to be over-ambitious. Henry Ellis stated, ironically as it proved, 'It is not at all unusual that a line, only costing £100,000 in making, had expenses which in the end came to three times that amount . . . The public is sick, sore and tired of schemes which put money in the pockets of solicitors, engineers and financiers'.

The B&E had the option of purchasing the CVLR within five years of its completion for a premium of 10 per cent over the cost price, or for 12½ per cent seven years after completion. It stipulated that the cost price was not to exceed £30,000. In return, the CVLR agreed not to extend to the LSWR without first seeking the B&E's permission.

The *Railway News* viewed the venture optimistically as the CVLR's estimated receipts were £10 per mile per week and 'the works are so simple that six months will suffice to construct the line'.

By 6th January, 1873, when a public meeting was held at the Star Hotel, Hemyock, about £10,000 of the £30,000 had been promised by shareholders. The Directors reported that they had deposited the Bill in Parliament and instructed Pain to set out the line. A total of £1,125 (five per cent of the line's estimated cost) was required to be deposited in the Bank of England on or before 14th January, 1873. Pain said that landowners now admitted that to bring their land into contact with a railway was certain to increase the value of their estates by 10 to 20 per cent. He reported that many landowners had consented to take the value of their land in shares. Pain continued by counting his chickens before the eggs were hatched:

> Although estimated earnings are £9 to £10 per mile per week, if they are only £8, this leaves £4 for shareholders [the B&E took half for working expenses - *Author*] and on 7¼ miles, £30 per week is £1,500 per annum, offering a return of 5 per cent on £30,000, plus perhaps £1,500 from rebates. The figure of £10 per mile per week was half the receipts

Notice displayed at the George Inn, Uffculme, announcing the first public meeting to consider a proposal for the Culm Valley Light Railway. Notice the alternative spelling 'Culme'.

Notice of meeting at Hemyock to receive report of CVLR Directors, 6th January, 1873.

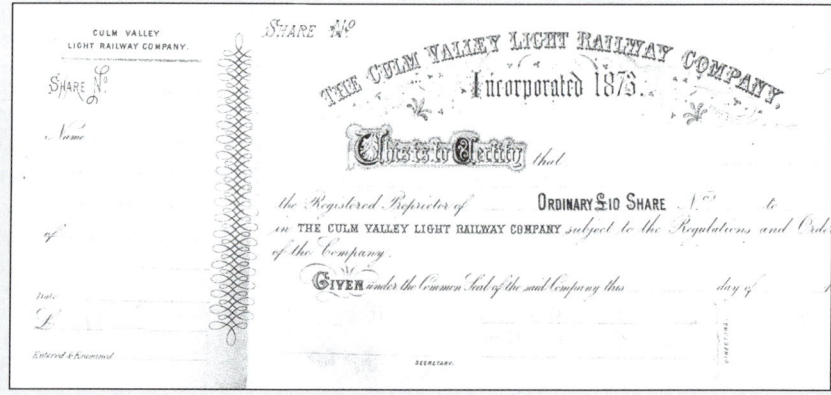

An unissued £10 CVLR share certificate.

PLANNING THE CULM VALLEY LIGHT RAILWAY

from the Chard branch and two-thirds that of the Cheddar Valley and West Somerset branches of the B&E.

Pain said that he believed the CVLR could be constructed for £22,500 with 'incidental expenses increasing it to £25,000'.

An advertisement for tenders appeared in June 1873:

No. of Contract	Description
1	Fencing. 21,648 yards run of larch, fir or wrought iron fencing, with gates, &c. complete.
2	Earthwork. The earthwork and ballasting from Tiverton Junction station to Selgar's Mill.
3	Earthwork. The earthwork and ballasting from Selgar's Mill to Hemyock.
4	Stone bridges. Widening one under bridge and the construction of two over bridges.
5	Timber bridges. Fifteen small timber bridges and 110 yards of tressill [sic] work.
6	Timber station buildings. Three small passenger sheds, three small goods sheds and one engine house.
7	Sleepers. 13,500 half-round larch, fir, or Dantzic [sic] pine creosoted sleepers.
8	Rails. 488 tons of 40 lb. rails, with fish plates and bolts, spikes and fang bolts complete.
9	Platelaying. Laying 7½ miles of main line and sidings.
10	Signal and telegraph. Six signals and 7½ miles of telegraph.

The contracts were awarded to:

D.A. Jardine, Hawarden, North Wales, Nos. 2 to 5 and 9 for £6,889 5s. 2d.
O.F. & C. Varley, Highbury, London, No. 10 for £208
Messrs Crawshays, Merthyr Tydfil, rails £5,612
Patent Nut & Bolt Co., London, rail fastenings £520
Burt, Boston & Co. London, No. 7 £2,210
E. Hernelewicz & Co., London, iron fencing £130
G.B. Sully, Bridgwater, wooden fencing £1,720 15s. 0d.
I.H. Langdon, Williton, No. 6 £1,207 10s. 5d.

The total price for tenders was £18,497 10s. 7d.

On 15th May, 1873 the Culm Valley Light Railway Act, 36 Vict. cap. 25, received Royal Assent. It authorized a capital of £25,000 with borrowing powers for an additional £8,000. Five years were allowed for completion and five roads were authorized to be crossed on the level. The line was to be worked subject to the provisions of the Regulation of Railways Act, 1868, but with a speed limit of 20 and not 25 mph. The *Bristol Times & Mirror*, 29th July, 1873, carried an advertisement for application for CVLR shares and said that 1,100 of the 2,500 £10 shares had already been subscribed for in the district. The CVLR Prospectus was issued on 25th September, 1873 and stated that 1,400 of the shares had been taken. It enthusiastically proclaimed:

> There can be no doubt, when the line is constructed, that a remunerative passenger traffic will arise while as regards goods traffic, the number of mills on the course of the line, into some of which sidings will be laid, the serge factories, and large brewery, the

BOROUGH OF TIVERTON.

CULM VALLEY LIGHT RAILWAY

To the Worshipful the Mayor of Tiverton,

WE, the undersigned Inhabitants of Tiverton and the Neighbourhood, being of opinion that the construction of the Culm Valley Railway will conduce to the prosperity of Tiverton by extending the sources of its Market, and thereby increasing its Trade, respectfully request you will convene a Public Meeting for the purpose of promoting the construction of the said Railway.

(Signed by)

Jno. Wills, Ex-Mayor	W. G. Chapple	S. Wright	Wm. Nash
Henry S. Gill, J. P.	Fredk. Wood	Arthur Paine	Jas. Creose, junr.
J. Lane, J. P.	John Blackmore	G. F. Burton	H. G. Sellick
R. Henry Taylor	Wm. Bartlett	R. Haydon	John Marshall
Francis Dunsford	Thos. Ford	S. Clements	Jno. Stevens
W. H. Reed	W. W. Martin	Herbert Sharland	James Mills
J. Heathcoat & Co.	H. C. Collard	R. G. Eastmond	Henry Rice
Fredk. Mackenzie	J. H. Cook	T. Williams	John Clapp
W. H. Dunsford	Wm. Cosway	John Cann	Jos. Wood
R. Duckworth	Jno. Ward	William Sheppard	John Coombe
R. R. G. Thomas, M.D.	Francis Ellerton	E. M. Winton	Thos. C. Haydon
J. C. Tucker	Francis Edwards Pike	R. G. Besley	Thomas Beck
	Van. Fisher	J. Bussell	

Having received the above Requisition, I hereby in pursuance thereof convene a Public

MEETING

TO BE HELD AT THE

Town Hall,

On Saturday the 8th February inst.,

AT THREE O'CLOCK IN THE AFTERNOON,

WM. NORTH ROW,
MAYOR.

Notice of meeting at the Town Hall, Tiverton, 8th February, 1873 to promote the CVLR.

Culm Valley Light Railway Company.

Incorporated by special Act of Parliament under which the liability of the Shareholders is limited to the amount of their Subscriptions.

CAPITAL £25,000,

Divided into 2500 Shares of £10 each; of which 1400 have been privately subscribed for in the district.

ISSUE OF THE REMAINING 1100 SHARES: Payable as follows: £1 on Application, £3 on Allotment, and the remainder in two calls of £3 each within six months, and of which twenty-one days' notice will be given.

The Directors do not propose to issue any other class of Stock, either Preference or Debenture.

DIRECTORS:

HENRY S. ELLIS, *Chairman, Fair Park, Exeter, Director of the Bristol and Exeter Railway.*
CHARLES J. FOLLETT, *Deputy Chairman, Poltmore House, Exeter, The Right Worshipful the Mayor of Exeter.*
WILLIAM BARNES, JUNR., *Great Duryard, Exeter.*
WILLIAM FURZE, *Mountview, Uffculme, Devon.*
EDWARD LUTLEY, *Whitehall Manor House, Hemyock, Devon.*
H. AYLMER PORTER, *41, Southernhay, Exeter, Vice-President of the Exeter Chamber of Commerce.*

ENGINEER:
ARTHUR C. PAIN, 5, *Victoria Street, Westminster.*

BANKERS:
THE TIVERTON AND DEVONSHIRE BANK, *Tiverton.*

SOLICITORS:
MARTIN, GREGORY AND BOWERMAN, 155, *Cannon Street, London.*

SECRETARY
FRED. POLLARD, *City Chambers, Exeter.*

HON. AUDITORS:
WILLIAM COTTON, *Exeter.*   JOHN CAVE NEW, *Craddock House, Uffculme.*

This undertaking is intended for the formation of a *Light* Single Line of Railway, on the ordinary (4ft. 8½in.) Gauge from the Tiverton Junction Station on the Bristol and Exeter Railway, up the fertile valley of the River Culm, through Uffculme and Culmstock, to a point near the village of Hemyock, as shown on the accompanying map.

The following table shews the distance of each of the proposed stations from Tiverton Junction :—

Tiverton Junction Station to Uffculme ... ... 2½ Miles
"   "   "   " Culmstock ... ... 5 "
"   "   "   " Hemyock   ... ... 7½ "

Below is given the names, population, &c., of the places which would be served by this line:

Name of Place	Population Census 1871	Distance in Miles from Nearest Station at the present time.	Distance to nearest Station on proposed Culm Valley Light Railway.
BLACKBOROUGH	152	4½ Miles	3 Miles
SHELDON	174	7¼ "	4¾ "
DUNKESWELL	557	5⅜ "	4¼ "
OTTERFORD	457	8¼ "	4 "
CHURCHSTAUNTON	822	7½ "	6 "
CLAYHIDON	728	5 "	2 "
HEMYOCK	983	6 "	Close to Village
CULMSTOCK	957	5 "	In Village
UFFCULME	1880		In Village
	6610		

The district which this Railway will serve comprises about forty square miles, and there can be no doubt, when the line is constructed, that a remunerative passenger traffic will arise, while as regards a goods traffic, the number of mills on the course of the line, into some

Prospectus of the Culm Valley Light Railway Company.   *Courtesy Tiverton Museum* of which sidings will be laid, the serge factories, and large brewery, the villages and farms it will run near or through, must ensure a considerable amount, consisting of Corn for grinding into flour, Hops and Barley for brewing, unmanufactured Wool, household and steam Coal, Lime for building and agricultural purposes, artificial Manures, Slates, Tiles, Drain Pipes, Bricks, Stone, Cattle, and foreign Timber, going up the line; Beer, Woollen goods, Flour, Hay, Straw, road Metalling, English Timber, Bark, Cattle, Meat, Butter and Cheese, coming down the line. It is estimated that the gross receipts from passengers and goods will amount to, at least, from £9 to £10 per mile per week. That this is a low estimate is best shown by comparison with the traffic on the following branches :—

    Chard Branch   (Taunton to Chard)   £20 0 0 per mile, per week.
    Cheddar Valley (Yatton to Wells)   £16 0 0 ,, do. ,, do.
    West Somerset (Taunton to Watchet)

The estimated cost of the Line, which has been prepared without any of the Engineer's items for Contingencies, is as follows :—

    7½ Miles of Railway, including Land and Stations ... £22,500
    Parliamentary and Professional Charges 2,500
                        Total Cost £25,000

Of this sum about £14,000 have been subscribed within the district, and the Engineer and Solicitors have entered into an arrangement with the Directors to carry out their work for a fixed sum, and take their remuneration in shares.

The scheme has been very favorably received in the district, and some of the largest landowners have agreed not only as to the sum to be paid them for their land, but have also offered to take the purchase money in shares.

The Bristol and Exeter Railway Company have agreed to work the line in perpetuity at 50 per cent. of the gross receipts;—to allow a rebate of 5 per cent. on all Traffic booked through and passing over their Line, and, in the event of its being considered desirable to borrow money on Debentures, to guarantee interest on such Debentures at a rate not exceeding 5 per cent.

The Great Western Railway Company have agreed to give for seven years a rebate of 5 cent. on all goods carried over their system (of 1,402 miles), and the South Devon Railway Company have also agreed to give for five years a rebate of 5 per cent. on all traffic carried over their system (of 120 miles), to or from the Culm Valley Railway. The importance of such arrangements with the neighbouring Railway Companies is evident.

The Directors of the Culm Valley Light Railway purpose, as soon as the Line is constructed, to concur with the Bristol and Exeter Railway Company in an application to Parliament for powers to authorize the latter Company to purchase the line,—within five years from the opening at a premium of 10 per cent.—and within 7 years, of 12½ per cent. on the whole cost, not exceeding £30,000.

As the name of the scheme implies, the Line will be constructed on a light scale—that is, the surface of the ground is followed nearly the whole way, whereby the necessity for expensive bridges, embankments, cuttings, and other works will be avoided.

In order to encourage the construction of this class of Railway, so valuable to Landowners and the country generally, an Act of Parliament was passed, in the year 1868, whereby power was given to the Board of Trade to pass light Railways for traffic, only limiting the weight of the engines used, and the rate of speed of the trains.

The permanent way will, therefore, be much less costly than on ordinary Lines, because the weight of the Engines will not exceed Eight Tons on each pair of wheels, and the Trains will not be run at a greater speed than Sixteen Miles an hour. The Stations will be of the most simple and economical kind, and the few Bridges required, being small, will be constructed of Timber. The works being so unusually light, the Railway will be opened in about six months after it is commenced.

The Directors have much satisfaction in stating that no promotion money has been or will be paid, and that they have received Tenders from respectable Contractors—in open competition—for the construction of the whole of the works, for a sum within the estimate of the Engineer, above given.

The preliminary expenses have been paid out of the Deposit for Shares subscribed in the district, and the Directors now lay this scheme before those locally interested, and the Shareholders of the Bristol and Exeter Railway Company, confident that, as the undertaking is thoroughly sound, the remaining shares will all be subscribed for and the capital raised privately, without recourse to financial agents.

The importance of such an extension as the Culm Valley Light Railway to the Bristol and Exeter Railway cannot be overrated, acting as it must as a feeder to the main line; and as it is promoted by the Landowners, Farmers, and Traders in the District, it is nearly sure to prove a safe investment for capital at a rate of interest of between five and six per cent. with the bonus above referred to, in the event of sale.

Applications for Shares on the annexed form, may be sent to the Bankers, or to the Secretary at the Offices of the Company, where Prospectuses and Forms of Application for Shares may be obtained.

                                            HENRY S. ELLIS, *Chairman.*
CITY CHAMBERS,   FRED. POLLARD, *Secretary.*
  Exeter, 18*th August,* 1873.

Prospectus of the Culm Valley Light Railway Company.   *Courtesy Tiverton Museum*

PLANNING THE CULM VALLEY LIGHT RAILWAY

villages and farms it will run near or through, must ensure a considerable amount, consisting of Corn for grinding into flour, Hops and Barley for brewing, unmanufactured Wool, household and steam Coal, Lime for building and agricultural purposes, artificial Manures, Slates, Tiles, Drains, Pipes, Brick, Stone, Cattle, and foreign Timber, going up the line; Beer, Woollen goods, Flour, Hay, Straw, road Metalling, English Timber, Bark, Cattle, Meat, Butter and Cheese, coming down the line. ['Up' and 'down' here refer to the gradient, not the railway terminology - *Author*.]

The permanent way will be much less costly than on ordinary Lines, because the weight of the Engines will not exceed Eight Tons on each pair of wheels, and the Trains will not be run at a greater speed than Sixteen Miles an hour. The Stations will be of the most simple and economical kind, and the few Bridges required, being small, will be constructed of Timber. The works being so unusually light, the Railway will be opened in about six months after it is commenced.

The population of the communities to be served were:

	1871 census	*1891 census*
Blackborough	52	76
Churchstanton	822	672
Clayhidon	728	480
Culmstock	957	854
Dunkeswell	557	344
Hemyock	983	877
Otterford	457	391
Sheldon	174	128
Uffculme	1,880	1,806
Total	*6,610*	*5,628*

The first annual general meeting of shareholders was held on 2nd October, 1873 at Godfrey's Railway Hotel, Tiverton Junction. H.S. Ellis, the Chairman, reported that the CVLR was viewed nationally as an important experiment in constructing a line for approximately half the normal price. It was announced that William Furze had taken £8,400 in shares and only about £4,000 was required to be subscribed. As soon as the £25,000 in shares was promised, under the Act the CVLR could borrow £8,000 so there would be no need to call up the whole of the £25,000.

In October 1873 the B&E subscribed £4,000 and in return was granted a seat on the CVLR Board of Directors, so in March 1874 John Walrond replaced Edward Lutley, who resigned in order to give him a seat.

Pain's report of 10th March, 1874 said that nearly all the land had been obtained and that the passenger and goods stations at Uffculme were 'in a forward state'. At the second ordinary AGM held at the Commercial Hotel, Uffculme on 19th March, 1874, Ellis gave an encouraging address. The principal landowners had 'parted with land on equitable terms'; there was no charge for litigation, but some arbitration fees would need to be paid and Ellis's *pièce de resistance* was that he believed that by the next meeting the line would be finished and open. The company held £4,000 in the bank plus £2,800 which had been received that morning. Apart from one or two exceptions, the whole of the first call had come in and the larger second call had been nearly fully paid. Ellis said he believed that the time was fast approaching when the B&E would pay the agreed 10 per cent premium and purchase the line.

The Culm Valley Light Ry Cº
To Rich Broome

1874

				£ s d
Nov 27	Railway fare & expenses Tiverton Junction to Exeter			4.0
Dec 6	do		Tiverton	2.3
16	do		Exeter	4.10
19	do		Tiverton	1.9
21 & 22	Railway fare Tiverton Junction to Nottingham & back to procure Locomotive			3.18.6
	Cab Bristol to Fox Walker & Co same purpose			4.0
	Hotel Expenses &c			17.6
	Various Conveyances			2.15.0
	Expenses incidental to Works One Month			17.9
	Telegrams			6.0
	Postage Paper & Envelopes			4.3
	Carriage of Parcels			3.3
				£9.19.1

Statement of Richard Broome, engaged to complete the CVLR.

Chapter Two

Construction

There is no trace of a date when Mr D.A. Jardine started construction, but it is likely to have been in March 1874 as the following month Pain reported that the earthworks between Uffculme and Hemyock were 'in a forward state' and that the contractor hoped to lay ballast within a few weeks. Rails had been rolled and were being delivered while the sleepers would arrive shortly. In June, Pain reported to the Directors that Jardine had informed him that the line would be finalised by October. Jardine had asked that photographs of local views be taken to decorate the stations.

This hope of early opening proved premature. In September 1874 Pain reported that although 23,000 cu. yds had been excavated from Crossways cutting just east of Tiverton Junction since March, 7,000 cu. yds remained. Good news was that the two brick bridges spanning it were almost complete; six of the longest timber bridges were finished and the remaining 10 were expected to be ready soon, as they were all of short lengths and the materials delivered. A wire fence had been erected at Uffculme and also the greater part of the timber fencing along the length of the line. The telegraph and signal equipment was 'in a forward state' and would be erected in a few weeks. Passenger and goods stations at Uffculme, Culmstock and Hemyock were complete apart from a few fittings. The revised completion date was the end of the year.

Jardine had opened a gravel pit at Craddock (between Uffculme and Culmstock); 2¼ miles of track had been laid out and this length was being rapidly extended and all the material, with the exception of some sleepers, was already on the ground. Of the £25,000 authorized by Parliament, £14,722 had been received in calls and the amount spent on construction to 30th June, 1874 was £14,827 11s. 8d. The estimated cost of completion was a further £12,286. Ellis told Jardine that his progress was unsatisfactory and that if matters did not improve, the contract would be terminated. Matters did not improve, so at the end of November his contract was ended and Richard Broome brought in as assistant manager, but not contractor, to complete the line.

The 1875 AGM was held in the Secretary's offices, City Chambers, Gandy Street, Exeter in February. Expenditure to 31st December, 1874 was £22,547 14s. 8d. and £836 5s. 2d. stood in the bank account. Receipts on shares to 31st December, 1874 were £15,536 and with loans of £8,000 and its interest of £27 19s. 10d. gave a total of £23,563 19s. 10d. received.

Although work had proceeded at a rather faster pace, Pain's report to the AGM told of delays caused by the very wet weather and in settling with landowners. Since the last meeting, the B&E had decided to lay mixed gauge on its main line and this resolution would be of immense benefit to the standard gauge CVLR.

To assist with construction, a driver and locomotive were hired from Henry Hind & Son, Nottingham at £8 per week. *Lizzie* arrived on 15th February, 1875 but needed attention. She commenced work on 20th February, but failed and was out of use from 17th to 30th March. Spare parts were sent from Fox, Walker & Co.,

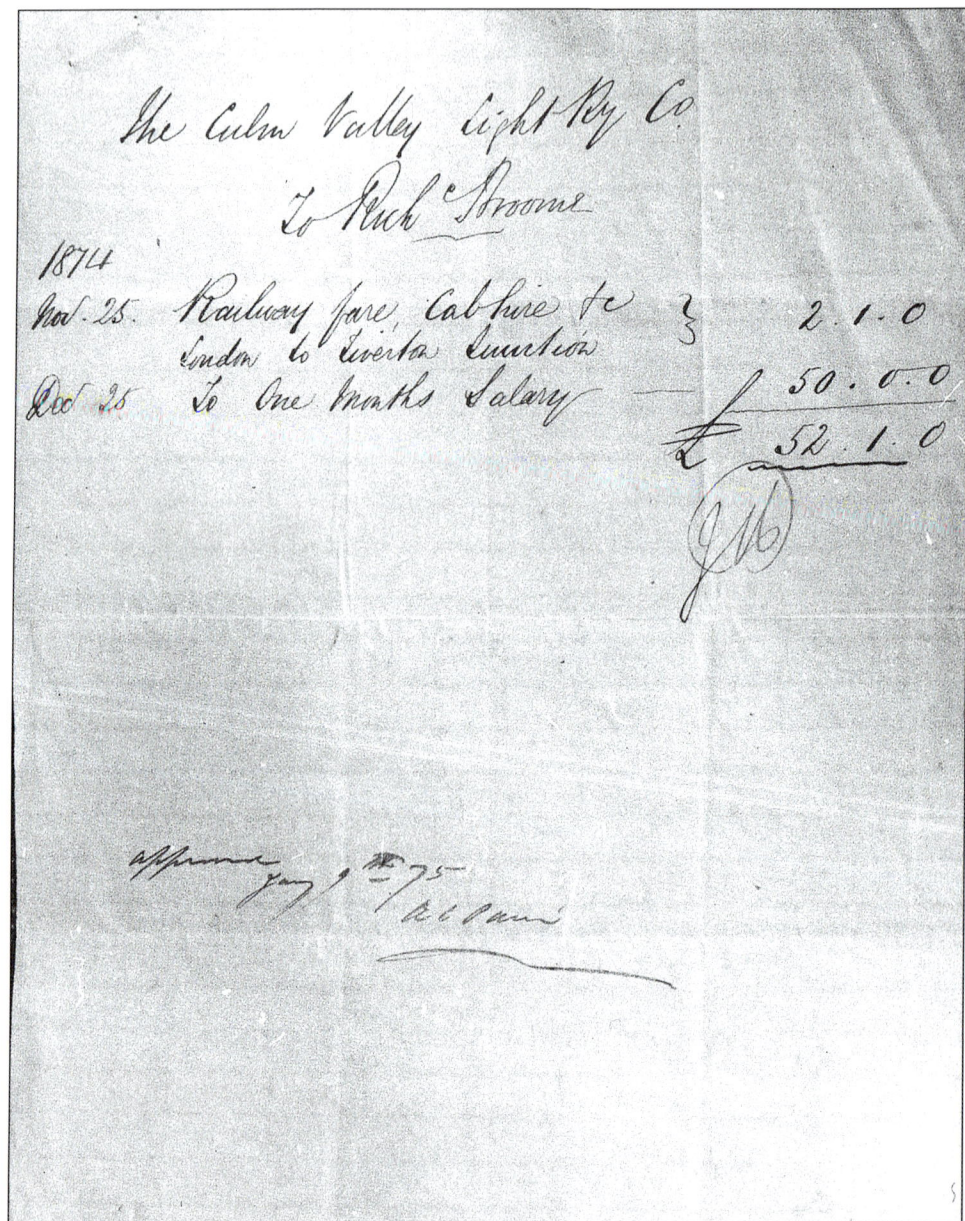

Statement of Richard Broome who was completing the CVLR, countersigned by A.C. Pain, Engineer.

CONSTRUCTION 19

Bristol, but *Lizzie* failed again on 10th April. Fox, Walker dispatched a fitter and she began work on 30th April. The CVLR made a substantial deduction from Messrs Hind's bill to cover both the cost of repairs and lost time. Hind's made the enigmatic reply that all new engines require constant repair. The CVLR additionally complained of the driver's 'incivility and direct disobedience'.

On 2nd April, 1875 unpaid calls totalled £1,212 - a sad blow to a company with monetary problems.

A special meeting was held in the Secretary's offices on 11th May to ratify the working and possible purchase agreement with the B&E. Ellis said that the line would be open in a few weeks, or at the latest, a few months, and the Directors would make weekly visits to encourage progress.

The first of these visits was made on 14th May and the Directors expressed dissatisfaction. Lack of progress was due to workmen, who also served in the militia, having to undergo training and thus not available to work on the line. A 'great pit' obstructed the railway east of Uffculme and needed infill to enable the locomotive and ballast wagons to reach Culmstock. Another cause for concern was that the permanent way in the Uffculme area was 'very shaky'. They commented: 'The Directors cannot help expressing their surprise that the Engineer has not in accordance with the Board attended the Visitation on this day'.

Broome's position as construction manager proved ineffective and in June he was asked to tender for the line's completion. He refused and so, from 19th June, 1875, the construction work was placed under Pain's direct control. Barnes, Follett & Furze made a comprehensive report following the 29th May visit. Crossways cutting had been broken through, though the sides needed sloping and the track ballasting. At Uffculme was:

> ... the most unsatisfactory part of the whole line requiring the most diligent attention of the engineer and manager. Large sums of money have been absolutely wasted on this piece of line; work has to be redone. To the casual observer no progress appears to have been made, the labour on this part of the line has been solely expended on perfecting raising and levelling the portion of the line hitherto supposed, but erroneously supposed, to be all but finished. Much to be done.

The pit near Uffculme had yet to be filled. Although no track laying or ballasting had taken place east of Culmstock, it was not expected to cause a problem.

On 21st June, 1875 the ballast engine failed yet again and it was two months before a replacement arrived. On 30th June £20,902 had been paid to the company and calls were £1,669 in arrears, including William Furze's £620 and Henry Ellis's £100. The Directors hoped to receive some return on their outlay by opening the line to Uffculme and thus capture some of the summer traffic. With this intention, on 18th May Pain wrote to the Board of Trade asking for a licence to open the line on 17th July. Frederick Pollard, the company Secretary, wrote to the Board of Trade in July:

> The Directors are exceedingly anxious to obtain before the official inspection after completion an opinion of the Board as to certain new features adopted on the line. This is a railway of a rather exceptional character and constructed with a view to reduce the expenditure on lines in rural districts.

On 14th July, 1875 the Board of Trade inspector, Col Yolland, reported that the line was incomplete, especially east of Culmstock. Although bridges were well-constructed, the 74 ft-long platforms at the three stations were too short and he insisted on a minimum of 120 ft. The branch platform at Tiverton Junction was too short and required a shelter. Points needed interlocking with signals while sidings required trap points. Curves of less than 10 chains radius required check rails. Col Yolland concluded that opening the CVLR could not be sanctioned without danger to the public.

The harvest in August brought a shortage of manpower, presumably due to the attractive overtime paid by farmers. At the half-yearly meeting in August, the Directors reported that works were still incomplete, but during the previous two months 'rapid strides had been made to completion'. There was excitement at Culmstock on 14th September, 1875 when the ballast engine reached the village for the first time and the inhabitants felt that they were really on the railway map. The *Tiverton Gazette* of 21st September carried the report:

> The ballast engine on this line bringing with it trucks laden with ballast was the admiration of the inhabitants [Culmstock] on Tuesday last [14th September] as it passed the Bridge. This was the first time it had made its appearance so near the village and shows signs of the approaching completion of the line. But there is yet such an amount of work to be done between Culmstock and Hemyock, that people are induced to believe the railway will not be opened in October next.

An incident giving an interesting contemporary view of the sanctity of marriage appeared in the *Tiverton Gazette* of 9th November, 1875:

> On the evening of the 5th instant [at Uffculme] a series of fireworks were let off and in addition to this, the effigies of the two married women and their husbands, the former eloping with two young navvies from the Culm Valley Railway, and the latter because they received them on their return after a month's absence as if nothing had happened. Several pounds had been collected for the occasion.

The edition of 23rd November, 1875 revealed that the elopers, whose effigies were burned at Tintant Lane, Uffculme, had again left, claiming that they were unable to bear being the talk of the town. The same edition revealed that tradesmen at Hemyock were anxiously awaiting the arrival of the navvies and looking forward to their spending power. Meanwhile, in early November, men in the CVLR ballast quarry at Craddock struck for higher wages. They had been paid 3s. 10d. a day. Pain offered them piecework, but refused to increase their pay and was more inclined to lower it to 3s. 4d. 'Many men left in consequence of the dispute.' The contretemps was apparently resolved, as we read in the *Tiverton Gazette* on 21st December, 1875 that, while working in the ballast quarry on the 15th, a quantity of stones and earth fell on workman Jennings. He was dug out by colleagues and escaped with only a bruised arm. Accident-prone, he had experienced several previous mishaps.

In November 1875 the Directors wrote to Pain expressing dissatisfaction at the non-completion of works. Regarding the financial side, by 31st December, 1875 £23,367 had been received and calls were £1,633 in arrears. On 4th January, 1876 Pain reported that ½ mile of rails had still to be laid and that ¾ mile of line at the Hemyock end required ballasting.

The Great Western Railway (GWR) had taken over the B&E on 1st January, 1876 and on 26th January the GWR Directors were invited to view the CVLR, but, due to delay in completion, this visit was deferred. At the AGM on 1st March it was revealed that the GWR officers had expressed the opinion that:

> Platforms of stations are insufficient and we say this from the conviction that the country around is so beautiful, and the attractions so great, a portion of the line going near the Wellington Monument, that there must necessarily be a large amount of passenger excursion traffic during the summer months.

George Nugent Tyrell, GWR superintendent of the line, explained that longer platforms were suggested because it was the intention to issue cheap excursion tickets from GWR stations once or twice a week. He also made the point that some accommodation must be made to cater for excursionists and hoped that tea, coffee and refreshments could be provided.

The *Tiverton Gazette* of 1st February, 1876 reported that the ballast engine had failed yet again and had caused men to stop work in the ballast quarry. Its issue for 15th February carried an editorial, embarrassing the CVLR Directors, but aptly summed up the railway's situation.

> *The Culm Valley Railway*
> It is a common question now-a-days to ask 'When will the Culm Valley Railway be finished?' The answer echoed back 'When?' Long enough ago promises were not wanting to assure the public that it was just on the eve of completion last Christmas twelve months and this light railway was no longer to be an idea in the engineer's brain, or merely represented upon sundry tracings and plans, but to be in actual working.
> Time has gone on and here we are in the year 1876 with the line cut, rails down, but the main point of carrying goods and passengers out of the question. It is much to be regretted this speculation should have encountered so many difficulties, for there can be little hope of its becoming a paying concern. If the original share capital had sufficed for all expenses incurred in its construction, the shareholders might have been spared from viewing the enterprise gloomily, but as we observe, application is to be made by the Directors to the Board of Trade for power to raise £10,000 additional as share capital, besides borrowing £3,000 more upon Debenture bonds or stock, it is not a promising out-look to those who have in many instances so generously supported the undertaking. It was simply upon the smallness of the capital that there was a chance of the line returning three or four per cent as an investment. If additional money must be raised, special inducements to capitalists will be necessary to induce them to invest, which will be felt by the original shareholders. We shall be glad to find when the line is open for traffic a brighter aspect - which present circumstances hardly warrant us to hope for - springing up before those who have spent their money in cutting the line, and that the good folks of Uffculme, Hemyock and Culmstock will become great railway travellers as an acknowledgement of benefits of the line. Since writing the above, information has reached us that there is some chance of the line being opened in March. The Government Inspector passed over it on Saturday [12th February, 1876] and gave a verdict in its favour [incorrect - *Author*]. This being the case, the question with which we started has at length received a satisfactory answer, provided of course that no unforeseen hitch turns up to delay the long-expected event.

A letter writer in the edition for 22nd February, 1876 sagely observed regarding the above editorial that although shareholders were unlikely to receive a good dividend, yet almost without exception, shareholders had interests in property, agriculture or trade in the valley or towns connected with it, so, due to the railway, would receive indirectly a very good profit on their investment 'probably in some cases twenty or thirty per cent'.

At the CVLR annual meeting on 1st March, 1876 it was thought advisable to increase the nominal amount of £7,000 agreed to on 30th August, 1875, to £10,000, plus borrowing powers of £3,000. This action was approved by the Board of Trade and laid before Parliament on 20th March, 1876. As neither House within six weeks of this date resolved that the certificate should not be made, it was formally issued by the Board of Trade. Unfortunately for the CVLR, the only investors to take up the offer were Edward Lutley who subscribed £20 and Arthur Pain's brother in Liverpool who subscribed £150.

Mishaps while the line was under construction were almost nil. On 11th April, 1876 the *Tiverton Gazette* reported that the foreman in charge of the erection of the school at Hemyock, after taking refreshment at Babb's New Inn, Culmstock, was on the platform at Culmstock station ready to take an illicit ride. As he attempted to jump into a wagon, he missed his hold and fell between a concrete wall and the locomotive, badly gashing his forehead. He was taken back to the inn where his wound was dressed.

Hind's ballast engine failed again in March and Ellis was forced to borrow from the GWR one of the standard gauge engines that the B&E had designed for working the CVLR. The hire charge was £3 a day plus fuel and wages. It started work in the week beginning 16th April. As the broad gauge line from Taunton to Exeter had had a third rail added which opened on 1st March, 1876, there was no problem delivering standard gauge (narrow gauge in contemporary GWR terminology) stock to the CVLR.

A view of Culmstock bridge from a brake van, 31st August, 1965.   *Michael Farr*

Chapter Three

Opening and the Early Years

Local people rather 'jumped the gun' regarding the line's opening. The *Tiverton Gazette* of 23rd November, 1875 said that the visit of the Board of Trade inspector was expected daily, while the edition of 30th November reported:

> In anticipation of the early completion of the Culm Valley Railway an influential committee has been formed for the purpose of obtaining funds and making arrangements for the opening celebration. It is at present proposed to entertain at public luncheon the directors and shareholders, to feast the poor, old and young, and to add the charms of music to what is eagerly looked forward to as an auspicious and happy day for one of Devonshire's lovely valleys.

At the meeting on 31st December, 1875 it was reported that works were incomplete, 'but in a sufficiently forward state to be inspected by the Board of Trade' - a curious statement because an inspector would not grant a certificate unless the line was complete. The *Tiverton Gazette* of 15th February, 1876 wrote:

> On Saturday [12th February, 1876] the new engine and passenger carriage of the GWR took the Government Inspector Colonel Yolland, the chairman H.S. Ellis, engineers, Mr Lutley and Mr Manley of Hemyock, from the Junction to Whitehall. Great satisfaction was expressed by all parties and arrangements are in progress for the formal opening in the early part of March, when the Directors and Shareholders will be entertained at a public luncheon at Hemyock. The Committee have engaged the services of the Tiverton Rifle Band for the occasion, and Messrs Withers and Wright, of Castle-street, Exeter, to supply the luncheon.

Colonel Yolland, however, reported:

> *Railway Department*
> *Board of Trade*
> *Whitehall*
> *14th February, 1876*
>
> Sir,
> I have the honour to report, for the information of the Board of Trade that in compliance with the instructions contained in your minute of the 19th ultimo, I have made a preliminary inspection of the Culm Valley Light Railway which commences with a continuous junction with a goods line of the Bristol & Exeter Railway at Tiverton Junction Station, and terminates at Hemyock Station. The length of the line, which is single throughout, with sidings at the four stations, Tiverton Junction, Uffculme, Culmstock, and Hemyock, and one intermediate, is seven miles and thirty chains, but the land has only been purchased and the works constructed for single line, and no arrangements have been made for addition of an additional line at any future period. The width of the line at formation level is 11 feet on the embankments and 12 feet in cuttings. The gauges were 4 feet 8½ inches. The permanent way consists of flat-bottomed or Vignoles-patterned rail stated to weigh 40 lbs per lineal yard in lengths of 15 feet, 17 feet 6 inches and 21 feet, laid on transverse sleepers of half-round Baltic timber creosoted (4½ in.), and 9 feet long, placed at an average distance of three feet apart, centre to centre,

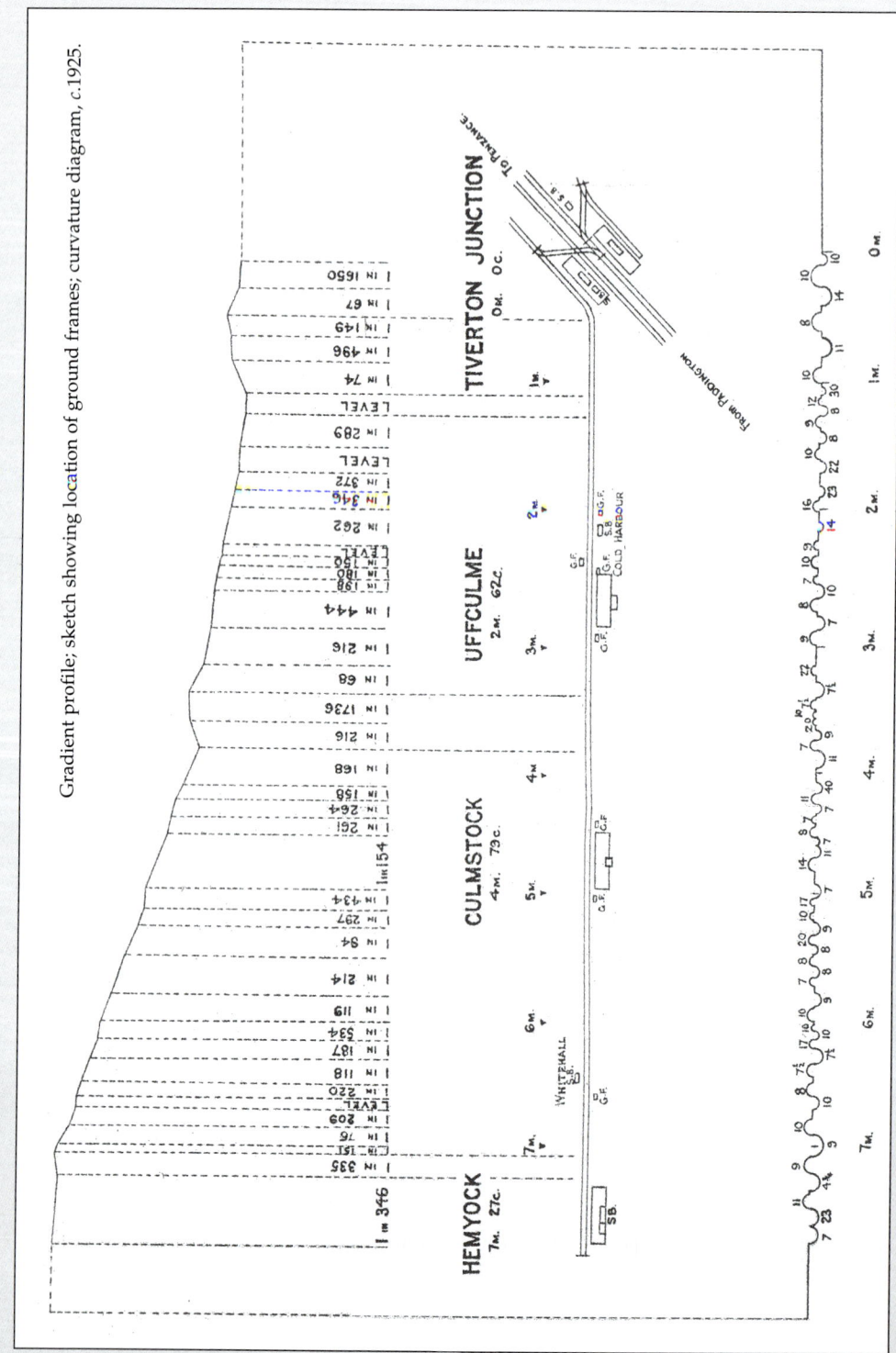

Gradient profile; sketch showing location of ground frames; curvature diagram, c.1925.

OPENING AND THE EARLY YEARS

except that on some of the sharpest curves an extra sleeper has been inserted under every 21 feet length of rail. No chairs are made use of, but the rail is fastened to the transverse sleepers by a fang-bolt with a clip under the head, overlapping the flange of the rail on one side, and by a wrought iron spike on the other side. On the sharpest curves a wrought iron plate is laid between the rail and the sleeper with holes punched in it, through which the fang-bolt and spike are driven; the joints of the rails are fastened with wrought iron fish-plates and bolts, and secured to the sleepers with a fang-bolt and clip on each side of the rail. The ballast is of gravel, a small proportion of sand; it was required according to the contract, to be eight inches deep under the sleepers, but is stated to average about one foot. No engine turn table has been provided. The line has a very large number of sharp curves having radii of 6, 7, 8, 9 and 10 chains. The steepest incline is one in 66.

There are three over and one under bridges, which (with the exception of one of the over bridges, an occupation bridge constructed of timber), are constructed of brick and stone or brick only; the largest span is 36 feet 9 inches on the skew. These are all substantially constructed, and appear to be standing well. There are also about 21 small wooden viaducts, constructed entirely of timber, over streams, brooks, &c, where the permanent-way rests on piles. I have not tested these, as the heads of these piles require to be braced together by other means than by transverse planking. The line has not been completed much beyond Culmstock station, at five miles up to the present time.

There are five authorised level crossings of public carriage roads. The platforms at three of the stations are only about 74 feet in length. I understood that the traffic is proposed to be worked by one tank engine in steam, whose weight is stated to be 20 tons 8 cwt. The other dimensions are given in the accompanying note, and I am told that the Company are willing to undertake that the speed shall not exceed 15 or 16 miles an hour, which was the condition assented to at the time by the promoters, that I recommended so many level crossings should be sanctioned. By some oversight, the limit inserted in the Company's Act is 20 miles an hour. Provision is also being made for working on the absolute block system. The undertaking as to the mode of working, description of engine, and speed, will require to be assented to by the Company which is to work the line, the Bristol & Exeter, now transferred to the Great Western Railway Company.

In going over the line I noticed the following:- At Tiverton Junction, the exchange platform which is to be used as the down platform for the Bristol & Exeter Railway, and the only platform for this line, is only about 7 ft 6 in. in width at the narrowest part. This width should not be less than 12 feet, and some shelter on it should be provided. It is only proposed to have home signals. These may suffice for a line of this description worked at slow speed, but the points leading into the sidings must be interlocked with signals, and the sidings must have catch points, to prevent anything being brought out without the consent of the signalman. Lamps and cross-bars should be placed on the gates at the level crossings of public carriage-roads where they are not situated at stations. The curves having radii up to ten chains, should have check-rails. The depth of ballast under the sleepers should not be less than twelve inches. The fencing is not yet complete throughout. Some of the telegraph posts, and one of the cabins at the level crossings, are placed too close to the rails. The gates are not yet all up. The platforms at three of the stations are too short. The officer of the Bristol & Exeter Company, who was present at my inspection, thought they should be long enough for six carriages. This would require them to be about 140 feet in length, but in the uncertainty which exists as to what the amount of passenger traffic may be, I think that if they are made 120 feet in length that may suffice. I have now, therefore, to report that, by reason of the incompleteness of the work, the opening of the Culm Valley Light Railway for traffic cannot be sanctioned without danger to the public using the same. I hope it will be found more convenient for the Company to withdraw their notice, and to give another when these requirements have been attended to, than for the Board of Trade to continue formally to postpone it from month to month, and I

Bristol & Exeter Railway
Engineer's Office
Bristol 22 May 1876

My dear Sir
                Exe Valley Railway

Mr Cooper informs me
that the train was expected
by Col. Yolland on Saturday,
and I do beg to the execution
I entertain regret events, he
appeared to be very pleased
for traffic on Wednesday next.
I think it will be recreation
Sir, what I have advised
your Engineer, Mr. Davis
(who has been guided by all
I have known of the line
& the Board of Trade its
requirements) amounted
to discarded as we accept
are for a careful and

satisfactory by Mr Davis
whenever I have arrived
matters when what is have
been in consequence
as to Mr. Davis, and I do
hope that as a result
say a few days Mr Hayter
may of health or not the
late weather decide when a
careful inspection — I will
state also the inspection will
take place during the course
of next week hitherto Mr
Hayter's engagements have
ensured upon as a much as
devoted to days up to London
in Select Parliamentary
Enquiry body.

Yours very truly
Francis J. Fox

Henry Ellis Esq
Chairman
Colsa Valleyhigh Railway
Water Park Exeter

OPENING AND THE EARLY YEARS

mentioned this course as the most convenient to the Chairman of the Company, Mr Ellis, who accompanied me over the line.

> I have the honour to be, Sir,
> Your most obedient Servant,
> W. Yolland
> Colonel

The CVLR sent a notice to James Grierson, General Manager of the GWR, to advise that the line would be ready for goods traffic on 1st May, 1876 and passengers on 20th May, though in the event the line was still unfinished on 1st May. As works were incomplete, the GWR provided, at CVLR expense: platform lamps, clocks at stations and signal boxes, furniture and ticket cases. Col Yolland made a further inspection on 20th May and reported:

> *Railway Department*
> *Board of Trade*
> *Whitehall*
> *22nd May, 1876*

Sir,
   I have the honour to report, for the information of the Board of Trade, in compliance with the instructions contained in your Minute of the 15th March, that I have re-inspected the Culm Valley Light Railway. The re-inspection has been deferred until this time in consequence of the Engineer of the Line, (Mr. Pain) having informed me that the LIne was not until recently in a fit state for Traffic.
   The requirements detailed in my report of Inspection dated the 14th February have been carried out.
   The Exchange Platform at Tiverton Junction has been improved, and some little shelter has been afforded - but an upright of the new footway bridge over the Line - and an Iron support for the railing of one under bridge under the Great Western Railway, is at present too close to the Line so that a door of a carriage could not be opened on the south side of the Line. The Line joins a Goods Line of the Bristol & Exeter Rly at this Junction Station and a throw off pair of self-acting Points must be put in to prevent Goods Trucks being pushed against the ends of the Passenger Carriages while standing alongside of the Platform. The Engineer has engaged to have these matters attended to at once.
   The viaducts require packing, as there is considerable oscillation in passing over some of them. This Company has to maintain the works for a year and I think it will be found necessary to have iron straps and bolts to connect the piles with the Longitudinal Timbers.
   The interlocking of the points leading into Sidings at the Stations with the Home Signals is of an unusual kind, and somewhat slight: in some instances these require adjustment.
   Name Boards, Lamps and Clocks are required for the Stations - the latter to be seen from the Platforms. At Culmstock Station where the Road to the Station Platform is across the rods for working the Points, these should be covered over, and at Tiverton Junction it would be better to work all the Points from the Box where the Block Telegraph Instruments are to be worked.
   Complaint was made to me by the occupier Mr. Brown of the dangerous character of a Level Crossing leading to Selgar's Mill near Uffculme, but the Engineer states that it is not a Public Carriage Road.
   There is no doubt that if there is much Traffic along this Road it will be subjected to considerable risk, but the Board of Trade has no powers to direct that a Gatekeeper shall

be placed there to attend the Gates. When the Siding alluded to in the enclosed letter is made, the Signals that protect the connection with the Main Line, can be made to protect the Road Level Crossing also, but until that is done, the approach to the Crossing from Tiverton Junction should be at *very* moderate speed, and the Engine Drivers should be instructed to whistle before approaching it from either direction.

I have not yet received the undertaking from the owning Company, concurred in by the working company as to the mode of working, rate of speed and weight of Engines by which the Traffic of this Light Railway is to be worked, but as soon as a satisfactory undertaking has been received, the sanction of the Board of Trade may be given for the opening of this Line for Public Traffic, as I understood from the Chairman and Directors last Saturday that they would carry out anything which I had to suggest.

I have the honour to be, Sir,
Your most obedient Servant,
W. Yolland
Colonel

Immediately following Col Yolland's inspection, the CVLR sent a telegram to Grierson:

> Colonel Yolland has inspected the Culm Valley Railway today. Report favourable to opening subject to undertaking which our Directors have given. If Board of Trade give sanction will you authorize Assistant Manager to open on Thursday morning [25th May, 1876]? Will write by post.

The line opened on Monday 29th May, 1876 and the *Tiverton Gazette* is to be complimented on the fact that it was able to print a description in its issue the following day, publication always being on a Tuesday.

> Somewhere about two years ago a company was formed for constructing a line of railway from Tiverton Junction to Hemyock. The scheme embodied the idea, that although the district was not a populous one, yet by cutting a light railway the cost of which was not to exceed £25,000 there would be a fair prospect for the shareholders receiving a moderate percentage for the outlay of capital. The line is to some extent an experimental one, for upon its success will no doubt depend the introduction of light railways into other districts, where the construction of more expensive lines could not be entertained. In completing the undertaking, the shareholders and Directors have not had all smooth sailing, several reverses in the course of work have gone against them, and necessitated an increase of the original capital set down in the prospectus, but after all the disappointments and the spread of many tongued rumours as to the time when the line would be an accomplished fact, the work has been completed: and on Saturday last, a train passed over the route depositing at the general stations, station masters, clerks, porters, and the necessary appliances for business. The line was opened for passenger traffic on Monday, and a special time table containing a list of fares has been issued by the Great Western Railway Company, (who work the line) for the guidance of travellers. The inhabitants of the district, through which the railway passes will have nothing to complain of in the way of accommodation. Five trains run either way daily, and first, second and third class tickets are issued by every train.
>
> The railway, which commences at the Tiverton Junction, and terminates at Hemyock, is seven miles in length, and passes through a good agricultural district. On leaving the Junction, there is a slight incline, and the train is soon brought into the only deep cutting to be found throughout the entire length. This being passed, the country is open, and the route is through a very pleasant part, presenting many attractive views. On the left,

peeping out between the dark foliage of tall trees, we catch a glimpse of Bradfield House, the seat of Sir J.W. Walrond, and shortly after, we are brought close to the River Culm, but passing over a wooden bridge it is for a time lost sight of. That we are approaching the first station on the line after leaving the Junction is evident from the sight of the central residences which stand in their own beautiful grounds looking out over the line ... After passing Selgar's Mills, and the factory of Messrs Fox, the Uffculme station is reached, situated on the right of the town, and from which a good view of the church is obtained, and also the noted brewery of Mr Furze. Here several passengers were added, and after detaching some goods trucks the train left the station. The line at this part curves considerably, in fact the entire route is as tortuous as it is possible to conceive of, and necessitates slower travelling than most people are accustomed to on a railway. Again in the beautiful open valley of the Culm, the train proceeds onward through some capital scenery, and shortly after a new brick building on the left hand side of the line, designed for the Culmstock School Board, betokens the approach to this once busy manufacturing place. Both the station and the place were gay with excitement, it being the anniversary of some club, the members of which, attired in their regalia, had assembled close to the station to watch the train come in. Flags were hung from the corners of the ticket office, and crossing the line was a banner, bearing the inscription 'The true Friends of Constitutional Liberty and Protestant Religion'. What connection this had with opening the line we cannot say. Did it refer to the Directors, or good people of Culmstock? The latter, ever anxious to further the interests of the town, met in procession some distance from the station with flags and banners, and headed by the Holcombe Regus brass band, playing 'See the Conquering Hero Comes', escorted the first train, 7.24 am, to the platform, when the crowd, numbering some hundreds of people, immediately commenced cheering. The band then struck up, 'God save the Queen' as the train left the Station, which was followed by another volley of cheers from the spectators, joining with merry peals given by the celebrated ringers of the town. At this station the tickets are collected, and we are soon on the way to the last station on the line. The Culmstock Beacon is a prominent object on the left of the line, standing out darkly against the distant horizon, and soon after passing this we get a view of the Wellington Monument. The tops of some of the hills in this part present a weird and barren appearance, whilst further down their sides and in the valley itself there is an abundance of verdant and luxurious vegetation.The train at length arrives at Hemyock the terminus of the line, and judging from mere appearance the question may well be asked what has a railway to do here? The station is some distance from the village and only a few houses show up, with just a sight of the church to give proof that it really is an inhabited place. At present much of the work at this station is in an incomplete estate, but is being proceeded with. Each of the stations has been erected near the bridges, which carry the public road over the River Culm, and forms a very pretty look out from these spots. With the exception of a portion of the line near the Hemyock station, it affords easy travelling, and the scenery throughout is exceedingly pleasant. Few, if any, places are so highly favoured with a special line of railway, as those on the Culm Vale [sic] Light Railway, and it remains to be seen whether the enterprise will meet with the support which it deserves from this newly opened up district.

Celebrations at Hemyock were not until Thursday 1st June, 1876; the *Tiverton Gazette* on 6th June reported:

Opening of the Culm Valley Railway
Rejoicing at Hemyock
This line was opened on the 29th ult., the auspicious event was celebrated at Hemyock on Thursday last, when there were rejoicings which will be long remembered in the history of this quiet little village. The terminus was decorated for the occasion, and in

CULM VALE LIGHT RAILWAY.

LUNCHEON, JUNE 1st, 1876.

MENU.

Boar's Head.

Galantines Veal.	Pressed Beef.
Hams.	Tongues.
Roast Beef.	Roast Pork.
Fillets Veal.	Raised Veal and Ham Pies.
Lamb.	Rounds Beef.
Pigeon Pies.	Roast Chicken.
Capons a la Bechamel.	Lobster Salads.

Noyeau Jellies.	Wine Jellies.
Chartreuse Jellies.	Russian Jellies.
Mille Fruit Cream.	Blanc Mange.
Gooseberry Tarts.	Open Tarts.
Fancy Pastry.	Rhubarb Tarts.

Ornamented Savoy Cakes.

DESSERT.

WINE LIST.

Champagne, qts. 7/- pts. 3/6 | Sherry qts. 5/-. pts. 3/-
Claret, ,, 5/- ,, 2/6 | Sherry ,, 7/- ,, 3/6

Port, qts. 6/- pts. 3/-

WITHERS & WRIGHT, COOKS AND CONFECTIONERS, CASTLE ST. AND MARTIN'S LANE, EXETER.

Chambers, Exeter.

Menu for luncheon at the opening of the CVLR, Hemyock, 1st June, 1876.

OPENING AND THE EARLY YEARS

the village, about a half-mile from the station, there were numerous tokens that the villagers were alive to the importance of the day's proceedings. Two or three arches - there are arches and arches be it remembered - were erected, flags were displayed, and the only motto conspicuous was at all events an appropriate one, and no doubt expressed the sentiments of the inhabitants - 'Welcome Friends' for perhaps it was but the outcome of an idea that now the railway is opened this picturesque spot will have a larger accession of visitors than has ever been the case before. The trains from the Junction during the day brought considerable numbers, Uffculme and Culmstock supplying contingents, who went to join in the festivities of their neighbours at Hemyock. These took place in a field opposite the terminus, the only division being the Culme [sic] which is a companion of the iron-horse most of the journey from the Junction. The Directors of the Railway, (in whose honour the luncheon was given), arrived by the train due at 1.25 pm. This hour was anxiously awaited, and a little patience had to be exercised, for it was nearly two o'clock before the engine was sighted, but in the distance the flags with which she was bedecked were plainly visible. A large crowd gathered around the station, and the approach of the train was made very evident by the explosion of several fog signals. The band of the 14th D.R.V. [Devon Rifle Volunteers], engaged for the occasion, struck up 'See the conquering hero comes', and when the Directors alighted they were received by the members of the Celebration Committee, and the Chairman (Rev. E.W.L. Popham), presented an address to Mr H.S. Ellis, (Chairman of the Company).

A certain amount of class distinction was evident. Luncheon was held in a large marquee near the terminus, while a dinner was given to about 250 working people of the neighbourhood in The Square, Hemyock, the repast provided by Messrs Walker of the Railway Inn and Mr Babb of the Star Inn. Refreshments were also provided in a field where during the evening 'rural sports and pastimes were indulged in'. A ball was held in the luncheon tent to music provided by W. Metcalf's string band from Tiverton. G.H. Braund, Tiverton, took photographs of the train, Directors and railway servants.

By 30th June, 1876 the CVLR had received £24,121 and arrears of calls stood at £879 and expenditure on the line amounted to £42,902 18s. 2d. The building cost of about £6,000 a mile was cheap and compared very favourably with other West of England branches: Seaton cost about £15,000 per mile, Sidmouth over £10,000, Ilfracombe about £10,000, Totnes, Buckfastleigh and Ashburton £14,000, the West Somerset £11,000 and the Exeter & Crediton £19,000, but this did not prevent the company's bankers from pressing for repayment of the loan.

The increased cost of the CVLR was due to:

a. The rails had to be contracted for when iron was at a high price;
b. The original contractor failed to complete the line and works had to be carried out by the engineer on behalf of the railway company;
c. Land cost more than was expected.

In July H. Cecil Newton, already holding posts of secretaryship to the Torbay & Brixham Railway and the Buckfastleigh, Totnes & South Devon Railway, was appointed assistant Secretary of the CVLR. It was a useful appointment as he had experienced problems of smaller railways having to deal with a larger company.

Railway Time Tables
FOR JUNE.

CULM VALLEY LIGHT RAILWAY.

FROM				a.m.	1&2 a.m.	1 2 3 a.m.	EXP 1&2 a.m.	1&2 p.m
Tiverton	...	...	dep.		9 15	12 20	3 37	6 0
Tiverton Junction	...	...	,,	6 50	9 35	12 40	4 30	6 45
Uffculme	...	...	arr.	7 9	9 54	12 59	4 49	7 9
Culmstock	...	...	,,	7 24	10 9	1 14	5 4	7 10
Hemyock	...	...	,,	7 35	10 20	1 25	5 15	7 34

FROM				12p a m	1&2 a m	12p. p m	1&2 p m	12 p p.m
Hemyock	...	...	dep	8 30	10 35	3 0	5 25	7 45
Culmstock	...	...	,,	8 46	10 51	3 16	5 41	8 1
Uffculme	...	...	,,	9 1	11 6	3 31	5 56	8 16
Tiverton Junction	...	...	arr	9 15	11 20	3 45	6 10	8 30
Tiverton	...	...	,,	9 47	12 5	4 30	6 51	9 20

CVLR timetable for June 1876.

UFFCULME, DEVON.

A QUARTERLY MARKET for the sale of Live Stock, Implements, &c., will be held in this town on the first MONDAYS of MARCH, JUNE, SEPTEMBER, and DECEMBER in each year.

The first of such Markets will be held on MONDAY, SEPTEMBER 4th, 1876.

Railway accommodation will be arranged for the transit of Cattle at the Uffculme Station.

A plentiful supply of hurdles for penning sheep will be provided.

By Order of the Committee,
WILLIAM BENNETT,
Auctioneer, Hon. Sec.

Dated Uffculme, August 3rd, 1876.

Advertisement in the *Tiverton Gazette* for the first Uffculme Market, 4th September, 1876.

Railway Time Tables
FOR DECEMBER.

CULM VALLEY LIGHT RAILWAY

FROM				a.m.	1&2 a.m.	1 2 3 a.m.	EXP 1&2 a.m.	1&2 p.m
Tiverton	...	...	dep.		9 0	12 20	3 37	5 45
Tiverton Junction	...	...	,,	7 15	9 35	12 40	4 30	6 30
Uffculme	...	...	arr.	7 34	9 54	12 59	4 49	6 49
Culmstock	...	...	,,	7 49	10 9	1 14	5 4	7 4
Hemyock	...	...	,,	8 0	10 20	1 25	5 15	7 15

FROM				12 p p.m	12p. a m	1&2 a m	12p. p m	1&2 p m
Hemyock	...	...	dep	5 50	8 30	10 35	3 0	5 30
Culmstock	...	...	,,	6 6	8 46	10 51	3 16	5 46
Uffculme	...	...	,,	6 21	9 1	11 6	3 31	6 1
Tiverton Junction	...	...	arr	6 35	9 15	11 20	3 45	6 15
Tiverton	...	...	,,	2 23	9 34	12 5	4 30	6 35

CVLR timetable for December 1876.

OPENING AND THE EARLY YEARS

The CVLR received a proportion of the receipts from all traffic passing over its line, calculated in proportion to the distance travelled, and for goods and minerals an allowance was made for terminal costs. Additionally a rebate was allowed on traffic passing to the GWR, South Devon Railway and independent companies worked by them. Half of the receipts was retained by the GWR as working expenses, while the rest was paid to the CVLR to service its debts and, in theory, to pay the surplus into the pockets of its shareholders.

In July a meeting was held at Uffculme to discuss the value of holding a quarterly cattle market in the town, as a result of the railway opening up grazing land where excellent beef and mutton were produced. It was decided to hold markets on the first Monday in September, December, March and June. The first market was held on 4th September, 1876 in The Square and over 100 head of cattle, 208 sheep and some pigs were sold.

Another development which could have boosted rail traffic was the racecourse at Uffculme, but the *Tiverton Gazette* of 5th September, 1876 reported:

> The GWR did not offer travelling facilities to intending visitors. For instance, a reduced fare of one penny with the disadvantage of having to wait several hours before the sports actually commenced, was simply a mockery of the public. Excursionists were few and most travelled by ordinary trains.

The weather did not help: due to heavy rain on the mile-long walk from the station to the racecourse, several feet of water had to be negotiated. The following year, the *Tiverton Gazette* said that the race was a purely local event and that no bookmakers were on the course.

Instead of the income of £10 per mile per week forecast in the CVLR Prospectus, the reality proved to be an income of just over £4. Total receipts for the seven months to the year's end were £1,015. Expenses amounted to £609 leaving only just enough to service the £360 interest on the debentures. Almost no money was available to pay the overdraft interest of approximately £600 and certainly nothing for the ordinary shareholders who had been promised about 5 per cent, yet had the line been built within the estimate, those shareholders could have received about 3 per cent.

The Directors' report of 7th May, 1877 showed receipts during the first six months:

	£	s.	d.
23,914 passengers	380	11	3
1,713 parcels	8	17	10
4,190 tons of goods and minerals	369	14	2
Rebate	58	6	10
	817	10	1

Expenditure on the line had grown to £44,852 15s. 0d.; the amount received £24,125 (£4 more than the previous year) and arrears of calls £875 (£4 less than the previous year). When the CVLR's bankers in June 1877 raised its interest rate on the borrowed £16,000, the loan was transferred to the National Provincial Bank, Exeter, where the CVLR's auditor was manager. The personal guarantees which the railway's Directors gave to the Tiverton bank, were transferred to the National Provincial.

On 1st July, 1877 Newton was appointed the sole Secretary at an annual salary of £60, but Pollard was to be paid £52 10s. 0d. in addition to the salary which he was owed, plus £15 a year for the use of his room still to be used for company meetings.

Unfortunately for the CVLR, the GWR was not proving too co-operative. Although the B&E had approved the initial plans and the Board of Trade had passed the finished line, the GWR seemed to expect the CVLR to be built to 'heavy' rather than 'light' standards. The GWR disapproved of the 40 lb./yd rail desiring something heavier; signals, level crossing gates, fences, ditches, and earth closets were criticised, as was the lack of lamp rooms and coal stores. Carriage steps struck the platform at Culmstock, but Pain simply slewed the track to obviate this.

On 22nd October the CVLR agreed to fund:

Trap points at the goods shed, Tiverton Junction
Low fencing to be raised to standard height
Pay £35 towards the cost of drainage at Crossways cutting
Cattle pens at each station
Widen goods sheds at Uffculme, Culmstock and Hemyock. (This involved moving one wall in each shed outwards by a foot, as hitherto the doorways had been only 9 ft wide. The doors themselves were suitably widened.)
3 yokes for lifting barrels from trucks, instead of altering the goods shed cranes
Replace 223 defective rails

The CVLR declined to instal water, in substitute for earth, closets.

The second six-monthly period showed a slight decrease in traffic over the first:

	£	s.	d.
19,949 passengers	305	15	6
Season tickets (no figures given)	5	12	8
1,709 parcels	12	12	2
3,731 tons of goods and minerals	302	13	0
Rebate	70	4	4
	696	17	8

It was now obvious from a year of operation that receipts were insufficient even to cover interest charges, so on 14th February, 1878 Pollard wrote to the GWR regarding it purchasing the CVLR. Two days later Grierson replied: 'The GWR is not desirous of purchasing any more lines', but added that he would be glad to submit any definitive proposals to his Directors. Figures for the second half of 1877 rose to 26,088 passengers; 1,969 parcels and 5,194 tons of goods and minerals.

Company Chairman Henry Ellis died on 13th May, 1878 and was replaced by Charles Follett with William Furze as deputy. As this affected the bank loan, William Cotton of the National Provincial Bank stopped the loan and it took several months to establish whether Ellis's liability ceased on his death. Eventually a new guarantee for the £16,000 was given by Barnes, Follett, Furze, Porter, Sir John Walrond and Mrs Ellis.

OPENING AND THE EARLY YEARS

On 16th July, 1878 Newton announced that he was moving to London to supervise the railway department of an investment company, the London Financial Association, but would continue as Secretary to the CVLR. The CVLR Directors agreed to the company's office being moved to 1 Drapers' Gardens, London. As the GWR had taken over responsibility for the line's maintenance, Pain's services were no longer required.

In 1878 'the depression in trade and the consequent low state of finances possessed by the heads of families' resulted in a substantial fall in the number of passengers carried. Receipts for that year totalled £1,716 and expenses only £915, yet the balance of £801 was quite insufficient to pay the overdraft and debenture interest, so on 7th January, 1879 a committee was formed to sell the line. Newton prepared a report claiming that the branch, if extended, could offer a quicker route from Exeter to London via Ilminster, Yeovil and the Vale of Pewsey - the Castle Cary to Cogload Junction line was about 28 years in the future. Certainly it was a shorter route and would have avoided the frequent flooding of the main line between Taunton and Bridgwater, but it was debatable whether the sinuous curves of the CVLR would have enabled it to be quicker than the existing climb to Whiteball tunnel and the route via Bristol. At that period the GWR and London & South Western Railway were engaged in rivalry between London and Exeter, the LSWR with its shorter route taking 4 hours compared with the GWR's 4¼ hours. However, the GWR was not anxious to purchase the CVLR and in May 1879 rejected the proposals.

The CVLR did not approach the LSWR for possible purchase as it was obvious that a line from Hemyock over, or under, the Blackdown Hills to Chard would have been a great expense bringing no advantage to the LSWR.

Looking around for other possible purchasers, on 23rd July the CVLR was offered to John W. Batten, a Parliamentary agent, for £33,000. As the CVLR did not readily appear to be a financial goldmine, on 29th September Batten and his friends declined to purchase it or make a loan.

A draft Scheme of Arrangement was made between the CVLR and its creditors to create £8,000 Debenture Stock A, £10,000 Debenture Stock B and cancel the unissued balance of the capital, making £10,000 preference stock and £3,000 debentures. This was approved at a company meeting on 26th September, 1879 but the proposal was overtaken by events.

The GWR was in an excellent bargaining position as it was not anxious to buy, but the CVLR very anxious to sell as it owed the National Provincial Bank £16,284. In view of the probable sale of the CVLR, in November 1879 the Scheme of Arrangement was abandoned and the CVLR Directors accepted the GWR's offer on 20th November, 1879. The GWR, which had taken over the B&E's investment in the CVLR of £4,000, offered a capital sum of about £27,000 to be paid in Debenture, Preference and Ordinary stock and sufficient to redeem the Debentures, discharge the bank debt and give a distribution of 5½ per cent among ordinary shareholders. On 2nd April, 1880 the half-yearly meeting of the CVLR shareholders approved this action and on 5th August the GWR's seal was fixed to the agreement and the line officially belonged to the GWR.

On 31st December, 1879 the CVLR account stood at:

	£
Share and loan capital received	25,170
Loans	8,000
	33,170

Income for the half-year ending 31st December, 1879 showed an increase of £39 15s. 6d. over the previous year's figures.

The last meeting of the CVLR was held at the London, Tilbury & Southend Railway (LTSR) terminus, Fenchurch Street, on 3rd November, 1882. It was held there because Newton had become LTSR Secretary in 1882. (He remained in this post until the LTSR was taken over by the Midland Railway on 1st January, 1912.) Charles J. Follett presided and also present were William Furze, Deputy Chairman; William Barnes, junior and H. Aylmer Porter, Directors; and H. Cecil Newton, Secretary. The Directors reported:

> The audited accounts for the 31st December, 1879, the date to which the accounts were last made up and approved by the shareholders, to the 28th October, 1882, are appended to this report. At the half-yearly meeting held on the 2nd April, 1880, an agreement for the sale of your undertaking to the Great Western Railway Company for a sum that would admit of the distribution of from four to five per cent amongst the shareholders was approved. The carrying out of this agreement has been protracted for a much longer time than was anticipated, in consequence of some difference of opinion between your Board and the Great Western Railway Company as to the position of that Company under its provisions. Without entering into the details of lengthy correspondence, it is sufficient to state that the Directors of the Great Western Railway Company have met the views of your Board with fairness and consideration, and have enabled your Directors to divide the full five per cent amongst the shareholders, which they would otherwise had been unable to do, and also to exceed that amount by one-half per cent. The duties of your Directors are completed, and as soon as the report and accounts now submitted have been passed by the shareholders, the Culm Valley Light Railway Company will, by virtue of the provisions of 'The Bristol and Exeter Railway Act, 1875' be dissolved and cease to exist.

Furze, in moving the adoption of the report, said that the company's main aim was to ascertain if a light railway running through a not very thickly populated agricultural neighbourhood could be made remunerative. The district was not solely agricultural, because there was a moderate sized town possessing a large brewery and several considerable villages on the line of the route. There was no doubt that the design as at first intended would have been successful, but as had happened in many other cases, the estimate put forth by the Engineer unfortunately turned out to be less than the ultimate expense entailed by almost one half. One cause that militated against them was the rise in price of materials, and a second was that the contractor who undertook the work failed, and it had to be placed in the hands of another. In consequence of those misfortunes the line took three to four times the period contemplated in completing, besides costing twice the money originally estimated. The receipts from traffic showed that if it had not been for those drawbacks the Directors would have been able to declare fair dividends upon the amount expended. It was first proposed that the line should be worked by the Bristol & Exeter Railway, and an arrangement was made that the company should purchase it, but the latter company became absorbed in that of the Great Western. In consequence of the expenditure largely exceeding the amount fixed upon, the Directors were compelled to raise money to finish the undertaking, and as they saw no chance of making the line pay, they were compelled to go to the Great Western company and ask them to purchase it. That company undertook to discharge all liabilities, and to pay a sum representing 5½ per cent on the money expended in laying down the railway - a very sorry return to the shareholders. When the arrangement was laid before the shareholders of the Culm Valley Railway two years ago to receive their sanction, there were certain points raised which had caused so much time since to be lost in winding up the affair. The correspondence which passed between the two companies was not so agreeable as it might have been, but in the end the Directors of the Great Western met the shareholders in a fair and considerate manner. The sale being completed, as soon as the meeting terminated the Culm Valley Railway Company would cease to exist. Although the shareholders present were few in number, he held in his hand proxies representing 60 persons interested in the undertaking to the extent of over £15,000. He moved that the report of the Directors, with the final statement of accounts, be received and adopted.

Mr Furze seconded the proposition, which was agreed to *nem. con.*, and the resolution was ordered to be sent to the shareholders and the Board of Trade.

Mr Barnes proposed a vote of thanks to the Chairman, and the same was seconded by Mr Porter, who also expressed the indebtedness of the shareholders to the Secretary for the valuable assistance he had rendered the company.

G.W.R.

Montacute

TO

HEMYOCK

Luggage label.

THE CULM VALLEY LIGHT RAILWAY

Uffculme *c.*1905 with the CVLR goods shed *right*. The open-backed locomotive cab has a protective storm sheet. The engine is a saddle-tank, probably ex-Whitland & Taf Vale Railway No. 1385. A signal arm can be seen to the left of the man seated on the pillar. Notice the timbering on the west wall of the station building. This was removed, or fell off and does not appear in later photographs. *Author's Collection*

No. 1300 at Hemyock. To the left is 'Hemyock Signal Box' and the round 'S' plate which was white on a red background. This indicated that the signalling was in order. If faulty, it was reversed to show a red letter on white. *Author's Collection*

Chapter Four

Consolidation and Growth

A potential for supplying the line with a good income was the Culm Davy Brick & Tile Co. Ltd, incorporated on 25th May, 1880. Its shareholders, apart from William Bailey, A.U. Higgins and two men from Exeter, included C.J. and R.W. Follett, both CVLR shareholders, Miss Nelly Follett and Cecil Newton, CVLR Secretary and also Secretary to the brick company. The brickworks were leased from the Folletts and the company anticipated being able to obtain a contract to supply bricks for the Severn Tunnel which was under construction from 1873 to 1885. However, the company's hopes remained unfulfilled and it was wound up in July 1881 and the siding lifted, though in 1878 flints used for road metal were dug near Whitehall and sent by rail to Exeter.

The GWR, after taking over the CVLR, began replacing the very light permanent way with heavier material and in due course the timber bridges were replaced by those of iron.

The Great Blizzard of 1881 had its effects on the line. Snow started falling on Tuesday 18th January and, by the afternoon, branch trains had ceased running 'the route being quite impassable owing to the heavy snow drifts'. It remained blocked until Saturday 22nd when it re-opened, but was then closed again owing to the effect of floods on Southey Bridge, near Culmstock station. The *Tiverton Gazette* of 1st February, 1881 recorded:

> The Great Western Engineer for this district, with a staff of men, visited the spot, and took the needful precautions to ensure safety, and traffic was resumed in the evening.

Ten years later was the even greater blizzard of 1891. It started on Monday 9th March at about 2 pm; the *Tiverton Gazette* of 17th March reported that some people at Uffculme '...could not battle with the storm and had to take shelter with friends for the night'. The snow continued to fall until 2 am Wednesday. The CVLR trains were cancelled on Tuesday and letters delivered on foot from Tiverton Junction to Uffculme, Culmstock and Hemyock.

The *Tiverton Gazette* said:

> The block on the Culm Valley branch was complete. The line was literally buried and to use an official's phraseology 'could not be found'.

On Friday 13th 'a large gang of men and snow ploughs were at work on the line' and the branch opened for traffic the following day.

In 1885 three Hemyock farmers, John Clist, Samuel Farrant and Edward Lutley discussed with butter factor James Wide ways of countering the agricultural depression. Unfortunately for the local farmers who depended to quite an extent on selling butter and cheese, refrigeration developed in the 1870s enabled butter to be sent from New Zealand and be sold in England at a competitive price. Another recent development was the centrifugal separator which enabled cream to be separated mechanically by steam power before being changed into butter.

CULM VALLEY BRANCH.

Single Line worked by Train Staff, and only one Engine in Steam at a time. The Train Staff Stations are Tiverton Junction and Hemyock. Form of Staff Square.

Section. Tiverton Junction and Hemyock. *No Train Tickets.*

Distance	DOWN TRAINS.	Week Days only.							
		1 A Mixed.		2 A Mixed.		3 A Passenger.		4 A Passenger.	
M. C.		arr. A.M.	dep. A.M.	arr. P.M.	dep. P.M.	arr. P.M.	dep. P.M.	arr. P.M.	dep. P.M.
—	Tiverton Junction	—	9 15	—	12 25	—	4 45	—	7 45
2 14	Gold Harbour Siding	9 26	9 40	12 36	12 45	4 56	4 57	7 56	7 57
4 62	Uffculme	9 49	10 0	12 54	1 0	5 6	6 7	8 6	8 7
4 70	Culmstock	—	—	—	—	—	—	—	—
6 34	Whitehall Siding	C R	—	—	—	—	—	—	—
7 28	Hemyock	10 15	—	1 10	—	5 17	—	8 17	—

Extract from the Regulations made by the Board of Trade for the working of the Culm Valley Light Railway:—

"That the said railway shall be worked between Tiverton Junction and Hemyock Station by one Engine in steam combined with the absolute Block Telegraph system ; that the rate of speed of the Trains shall not exceed fifteen miles an hour on any part of the said Railway ; and that the Locomotive Engines, Carriages and Vehicles used on the Railway shall not have a greater weight than eight tons upon the rails upon any one pair of wheels."

Wagons for Cold Harbour Siding to be worked by Special Goods from Tiverton Junction,

Distance	UP TRAINS.	Week Days only.							
		1 A Passenger.		2 A Mixed.		3 A Mixed.		4 A Passenger.	
M. C.		arr. A.M.	dep. A.M.	arr. A.M.	dep. A.M.	arr. P.M.	dep. P.M.	arr. P.M.	dep. P.M.
—	Hemyock	—	8 15	—	10 45	—	2 55	—	5 45
— 74	Whitehall Siding	—	—	C R	—	—	—	—	—
2 29	Culmstock	—	—	—	—	—	—	—	—
4 46	Uffculme	8 25	8 26	10 55	11 1	3 5	3 11	5 55	5 56
5 14	Cold Harbour Siding	8 35	8 37	11 10	11 16	3 20	3 25	6 5	6 7
7 28	Tiverton Junction	8 48	—	11 30	—	3 37	—	6 18	—

Above: Working timetable July 1898.

Left: A Culm Davy brick.

CONSOLIDATION AND GROWTH 41

Culmstock level crossing view north. *Amyas Crump Collection*

Culmstock level crossing view north. *Amyas Crump Collection*

THE CULM VALLEY LIGHT RAILWAY

Ex-Watlington & Princes Risborough Railway No. 2 as GWR No. 1384 at Hemyock c.1908 with ex-Manchester & Milford Railway coaches. The cattle pen is on the right, the River Culm on the far right. Notice the flat-bottomed rail. The hampers are lettered 'A. Wide'. James Wide was a butter factor at Hemyock. Someone is seated on the floor of the first coach with their feet on the running board. *Author's Collection*

The Culm Valley Dairy Company's siding c.1905. *Author's Collection*

CONSOLIDATION AND GROWTH

This method was eminently suited to economic large scale production, impossible by using the old manual method. Thus in 1886 the Culm Valley Dairy Company was formed at Clist's Farm, Mountshayne, south of Hemyock. It was the first mechanised butter factory in the West of England and its product was dispatched by rail all over Britain. The factory opened on 16th May, 1886 and that month dealt with 3,000 gallons of milk and this increased by May 1890 to over 100,000 gallons. A by-product was skimmed milk. This was fed to pigs and soon a pig market was started at Hemyock and provided yet more rail traffic, while 1888 saw an animal feedstuffs mill being developed at Culmstock to provide additional food for the piggeries.

Butter manufacture increased to such an extent that new premises were required and these were found at Millhayes Mill, which had a railway siding. It continued to produce cattle feed and a butter and cheese factory were added. The factory's products were dispatched by passenger train and in 1903 Hemyock station took about £1,200 in parcels traffic receipts, much of it coming from this factory.

Statistics for 1903 reveal that over a third of the traffic received on the branch was coal. Uffculme was the busiest goods station on the branch followed by Hemyock, but ticket sales at Culmstock were greater than at Hemyock. Uffculme and Culmstock stations each had a staff of four and there were three at Hemyock. The wage bill for the year was £513.

By 1913 goods train traffic had doubled. This was due to 6,750 tons of 'other minerals' being forwarded, the largest proportion of this being stone from a quarry at Coombe Hill, north of Hemyock. In 1911 James Yates had set up the Hemyock Stone & Coal Co. Ltd to develop his business. It was rather a 'flash in the pan' affair and in 1916 Yates was appointed as the company's liquidator. By 1913 cattle traffic had more than doubled to 217 wagons a year. Staff changes on the branch left Uffculme with three, Hemyock with five and Culmstock with only one man as it was controlled from Tiverton Junction. The branch wage bill was £529 per annum.

In 1916 Wilts United Dairies acquired the Culm Valley Dairy for £9,000. It ceased manufacturing butter and concentrated on liquid milk for the London market. In 1920 a new factory opened at Hemyock for producing condensed milk and, to ease transport problems, the line serving the passenger platform was extended across the road to this new building. It was for this factory that two boilers weighing 26 tons each were constructed at Wolverhampton. Because the wagons carrying them would have been too long, and therefore on the prohibited list for the branch, the GWR declined to convey them and so they had to be sent by road.

From 1922 to 1928 United Dairies leased the factory to Milkal Ltd, a subsidiary of J. Lyons & Co., to produce spray-dried milk and spray-dried ice cream powder. This caused branch receipts to fall in 1925 by £2,043 because liquid milk was sent by passenger train, but dried milk went by goods at a lower rate.

In 1927 United Dairies used the first rail bulk milk tanks to run in England, hitherto all such traffic had been in 17 gallon churns weighing 2¼ cwt when full. Tanks were more economical than churns. One man could rinse a tank with cold water and scrub it, gaining access through a manhole. It was then rinsed with hot water and finally sterilised with steam - a much easier option than

Left: Hemyock view west c.1912. The carriage shed can be seen above the roof of the nearest coach, with the engine shed on the far left. The coal wagon is from West Cannock Colliery. *Author's Collection*

Below: Working timetable June 1914.

CULM VALLEY BRANCH.

Single Line worked by Train Staff and only one Engine in Steam at a time. The Train Staff Stations are Tiverton Junction and Hemyock.

Distance		Station No.	DOWN TRAINS.	1 B Mixed.		2 B Mixed.		Week Days only. 3 K Goods.		4 B Passenger.		5 B Passenger.	
M.	C.			arr. A.M.	dep. A.M.	arr. P.M.	dep. P.M.	arr. P.M.	dep. P.M.	arr. P.M.	dep. P.M.	arr. P.M.	dep. P.M.
—	—	1538	Tiverton Junction	—	9 15	—	12 27	—	4 0	—	5 20	—	7 42
2	14	1610	Cold Harbour Siding	9 27	9 42	12 39	12 47	CR	4 12	—	—	—	7 55
2	62	1611	Uffculme	9 51	10 6	12 58	1 7	RR	—	—	5 33	—	8 6
4	79	1612	Culmstock	CR	—	—	—	—	—	—	5 43	—	—
6	34	1613	Whitehall Siding	—	—	—	—	—	—	—	—	—	—
7	27	1615	Hemyock	10 20	—	1 17	—	Q	—	5 53	—	8 15	—

Q To be run when Mixed trains cannot clear traffic. Not to be run with less than 3 wagons.

	UP TRAINS.	1 B Passenger.		2 B Mixed.		Week Days only. 3 B Mixed.		4 K Goods.		5 B Passenger.	
		arr. A.M.	dep. A.M.	arr. A.M.	dep. A.M.	arr. P.M.	dep. P.M.	arr. P.M.	dep. P.M.	arr. P.M.	dep. P.M.
	Hemyock	—	8 10	—	10 45	—	2 55	—	RR	—	6 0
	Whitehall Siding	—	—	—	CR	—	—	—	—	—	—
	Culmstock	—	—	8 21	—	3 5	3 10	—	—	6 10	6 12
	Uffculme	—	—	10 55	11 1	3 19	3 24	—	—	6 21	6 23
	Cold Harbour Sdg	8 30	—	11 10	11 18	CR	—	—	4 25	—	—
	Tiverton Junct.	8 44	—	11 30	—	3 36	—	—	4 37	6 35	—

Extract from the Regulations made by the Board of Trade for the working of the Culm Valley Light Railway:—
"This railway shall be worked between Tiverton Junction and Hemyock Station by means of one Engine in steam carrying the staff; that the rate of speed of the Trains shall not exceed fifteen miles an hour on any part of the said Railway; and that the Locomotive Engines, Carriages and Vehicles used on the Railway shall not have a greater weight than eight tons upon the rails on any one pair of wheels."
Long Round Timber.—Long Round Timber must not be accepted for transit at Uffculme, Culmstock or Hemyock. Wagons for Cold Harbour Siding to be worked by Special Goods from Tiverton Junction.

CONSOLIDATION AND GROWTH 45

Uffculme c.1930: level crossing; goods yard, *left*, with cattle vans at the cattle dock; two of George Small's carts in the yard loaded with sacks, and a third soon to turn into the yard. William Furze's brewery is on the right skyline. On the far right a GWR Thorneycroft lorry can just be seen.
Author's Collection

Hemyock before the 1920 track alterations and building extension. Note the flat-bottomed rail, cattle dock and carriage shed.
Author's Collection

carrying out these procedures with the 176 seventeen gallon churns which held the equivalent of one tank. The 176 churns needed three vans to carry them and weighed a total of 80 tons, whereas one tank wagon was only 22 tons. The 3,000 gallon enamel glass-lined tanks were manufactured by the Dairy Supply Company, and the chassis was built at Swindon. Each tank was insulated with a 2 in. layer of cork. From 1932 United Dairies used these 6-wheel milk tanks to carry milk from Hemyock and they were the only 6-wheelers permitted to run over the branch. The dairy owned the actual milk tanks, while the railway owned and maintained the underframe, axleboxes being topped up at Exeter, though in the final years of the branch this operation was carried out at Hemyock daily. Initially milk was collected from local farms by horse and cart, but latterly the milk depot had a fleet of about a dozen lorries. Usually half a dozen 3,000 gallon tank wagons were sent to depots at Wood Lane, Vauxhall and Ilford daily, but sometimes the numbers rose to 12.

Due to the reduced number of hours worked weekly, in 1923 branch staff totalled 13: four at Uffculme, two at Culmstock and seven at Hemyock, with the wages bill standing at a hefty £1,863 - more than three times the amount it had been 10 years previously. In 1925 branch receipts were £22,069 and expenses £7,857, giving a profit of £14,752.

During the General Strike no trains were run from midnight Monday 3rd May, 1926 until the strike was settled on Wednesday 12th May. The people of Hemyock were seriously inconvenienced by the strike as no train ran, whereas in that of 1919 a skeleton service was operated. In 1928 inwards traffic to Hemyock dairy included coal and New Zealand butter, the latter blended with local product. Outwards traffic from the branch was meat and farm produce including hampers of rabbits. In 1933 only 10 staff were employed on the branch: four each at Uffculme and Hemyock and two at Culmstock, the total wages bill amounting to £1,159.

An early view of Hemyock with the former refreshment room behind and slightly to the right. The three-compartment coaches can be seen on the left, notice the casing for the pot-type oil lamps above their roofs. The gate in the foreground gave access to the bank of the River Culm. *Author's Collection*

Chapter Five

Description of the Line

Tiverton Junction, 179 miles from Paddington and 15 miles from Exeter, opened on 1st May, 1844 as Tiverton Road. With the opening of the branch to Tiverton itself, on 12th June, 1848, it was renamed Tiverton Junction. As the Taunton to Exeter line became mixed gauge on 1st March, 1876, from its opening on 29th May, 1876 the CVLR had immediate access to and from the national system.

With the construction of the CVLR, Tiverton Junction's down platform was made into an island on which stood the Culm Valley Branch signal box. A short spur at the east end of the branch platform enabled gravity shunting to be employed to run the engine round. After passengers had been detrained, the engine propelled its coaches up the gradient towards Hemyock; the guard would apply his brake, uncouple the coaches from the engine which would then run into the spur to allow the guard to let the coaches drift down into the platform where the engine could be re-coupled at the Hemyock end of the train.

To improve traffic flow on the main line, track was quadrupled through the station in 1932 under a Government Loan Scheme. Non-stop trains used the centre through roads, while stopping trains used the platform roads. The new track layout enabled Culm Valley trains to use either face of the down platform and run round trains without using gravity - in fact this method could no longer be used because the spur had been removed. At the time of quadrupling the goods and engine sheds were rebuilt. In the former were kept re-railing ramps and two screw couplings.

In 1880 the Duchess of Devonshire Dairy had opened north-west of the station and rail was used for the dispatch of cardboard boxes of butter and cheese, each containing 28lb. This traffic peaked at 231,160 boxes in 1923. Imported butter arrived in 56 lb. boxes for blending with the local product. Twenty platform trolleys could be under load with butter at any one time. The factory had over 100 employees in the 1920s and 1930s, but closed in 1960.

About 1910 Lloyd Maunder's slaughterhouse was established in the fork between the Tiverton branch and the main line. Cattle, sheep and pigs arrived by rail, 1,645 wagons in 1929, while meat was dispatched in refrigerated vans, mostly to Smithfield Market. The goods shed sent out slaughterhouse by-products such as bones.

Tiverton Junction received animal feedstuffs for Messrs Silcocks who kept their stock in a lock-up at one end of the Tiverton Junction goods shed. The feed was distributed by GWR country lorry service.

When hampers of dead rabbits were on a Culm Valley train, at Uffculme the guard advised Tiverton Junction of their imminent arrival so that barrows could be organised to carry the consignment from the branch platform across to the up main line platform for onwards transit to London. Each barrow could hold about 24 crates.

Tiverton Junction had a full range of facilities and apart from dealing with ordinary passenger and goods traffic, having carriage and cattle docks it could handle specialised traffic. In 1904 the yard had an 8 ton crane, but by 1956 the capacity was 6 tons - possibly the same crane downgraded.

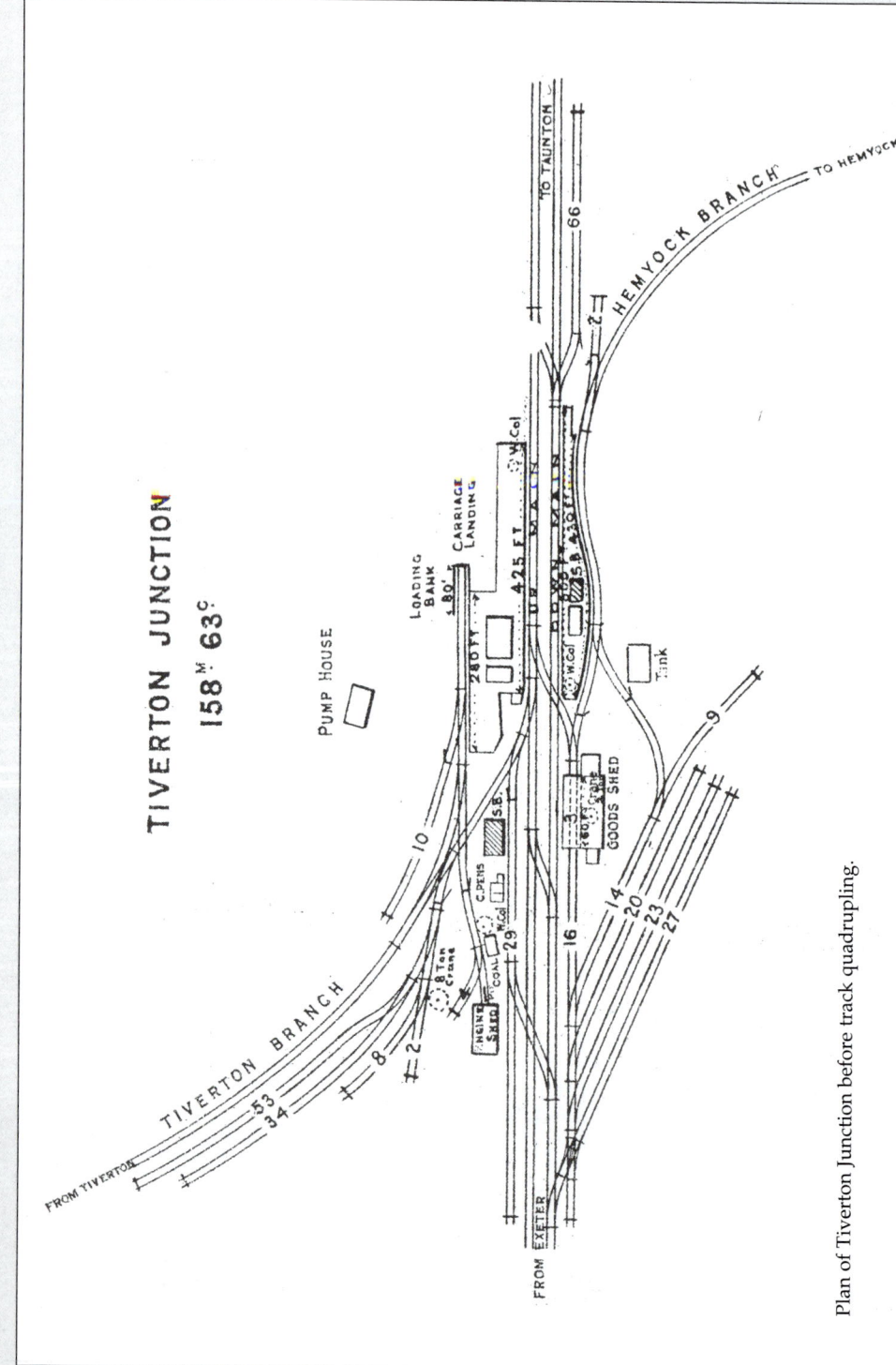

Plan of Tiverton Junction before track quadrupling.

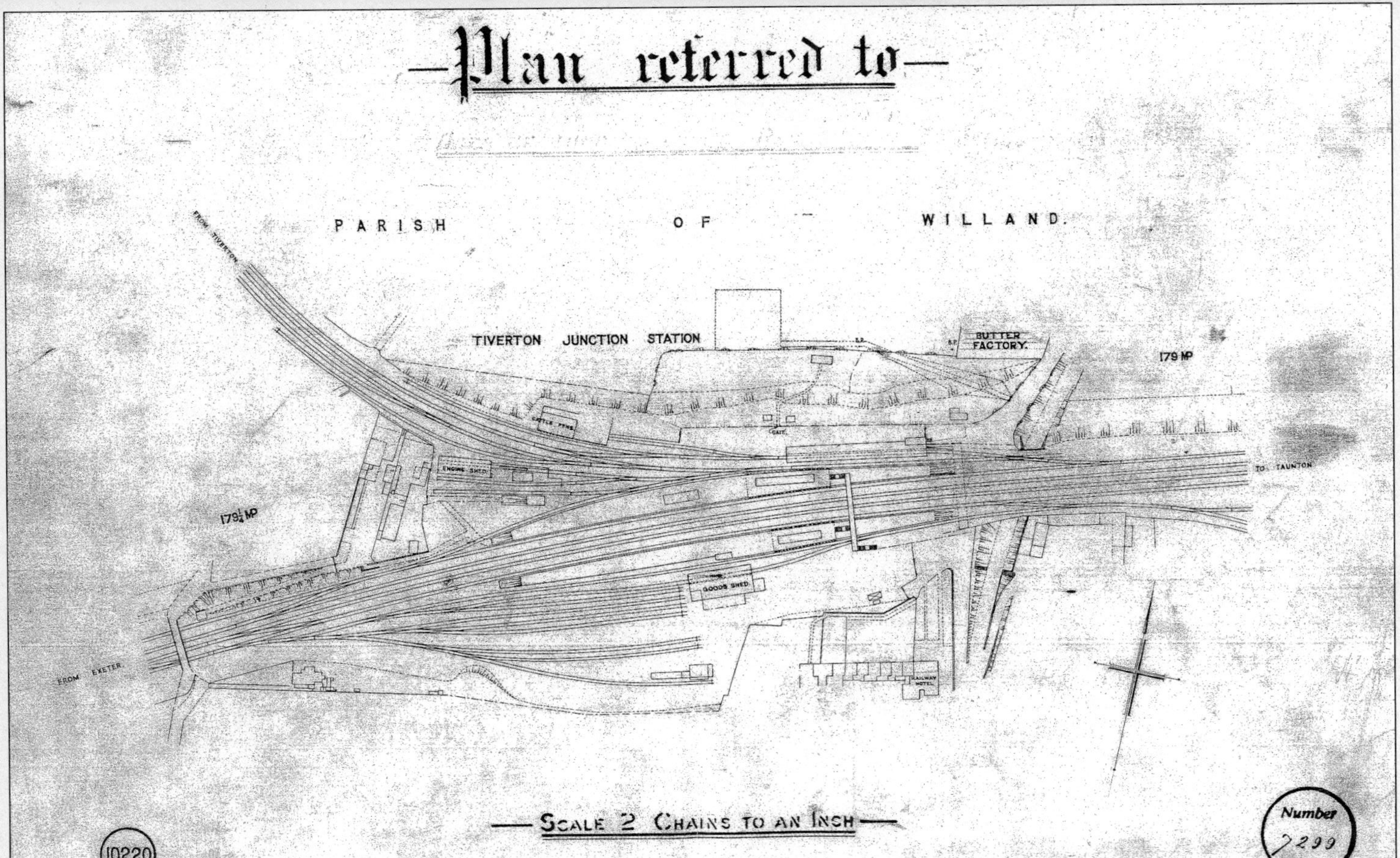
Plan referred to
PARISH OF WILLAND.
FROM TIVERTON
TIVERTON JUNCTION STATION
BUTTER FACTORY.
179 MP
CATTLE PENS
GATE
ENGINE SHED
TO TAUNTON
179¼ MP
GOODS SHED
RAILWAY HOTEL
FROM EXETER
SCALE 2 CHAINS TO AN INCH
10220
9.45
Number
7299

Plan of Tiverton Junction after track quadrupling.

Tiverton Junction, 1921, in double track days, view down. A Hemyock branch train can be seen, *left*, and the goods shed *centre*, with the original engine shed beyond the end of the up platform.
Lens of Sutton

View up, 28th January, 1932. The Hemyock branch platform is on the far right. Notice the water crane.
Author's Collection

DESCRIPTION OF THE LINE

Staff in 1925 numbered 25: station master, three clerks, one ticket collector, three parcel porters, four porters, one goods checker, one goods porter, three shunters (early, late and night turns), five signalmen (two at Sampford Siding), two guards and one charwoman. About 1930 the goods guards previously based at Hemyock came under the Tiverton Junction station master. In 1919, following the closure of Hemyock shed, Tiverton Junction had four sets of enginemen plus a shedman who spent the night cleaning and preparing the engines.

Early in 1879 at the suggestion of Sir John Walrond Bt, the GWR Directors sanctioned holding two religious services a month in the waiting room of Tiverton Junction as the parish church at Willand was almost a mile distant.

Apart from mineral and general goods traffic, from 18th November, 1943 the station had Park Sidings used by the Anglo-American Oil Company to supply petrol to the Air Ministry's storage tanks east of the station. Out of use in 1947 they were brought back into use in 1961, fuel arriving in block trains from Avonmouth and Fawley. This depot closed on 30th April, 1983 while Tiverton Junction had closed to general goods traffic on 8th May, 1967. The opening on 12th May, 1986 of Tiverton Parkway station 1¾ miles to the north caused the closure of the former Tiverton Junction station, though due to engineering work over the weekend, the last train to call was on Friday 9th May. Tiverton Junction site is now used for car sales and a lorry maintenance depot.

On leaving the Junction the branch almost immediately traversed a 10 chain radius curve through 90° on a rising gradient of 1 in 67 for 25 chains. Some 517 yards from the Junction, up (from Hemyock) goods trains were required to halt at a Stop Board to ensure that they were under control. Drivers had to be aware that shunting could be taking place ahead of the home signal, though occupation of the Culm Valley branch line should not have taken place after a train had left Uffculme for Tiverton Junction.

Immediately beyond the Stop Board the line passed below a three-span timber bridge carrying a footpath over Crossways cutting. By 1951 the timber had decayed and the bridge was leaning, so was replaced by a reinforced concrete span of 50 ft. Crossways cutting was also spanned by two adjacent brick bridges, still extant. The first carries the road to Halberton and the second, the B3181, formerly the A38.

The line fell at 1 in 149/496/74 for 27 chains and while descending near Jaycroft Farm encountered an eight chain curve through 90°. Near mile post 1 the line reached the foot of the Culm Valley which it followed to Hemyock, the trend being an upward gradient. Selgar's Mill was passed and beyond, the leat feeding it was crossed on the skew by a riveted iron bow-string girder bridge. A facing siding (2 miles 14 chains from Tiverton Junction), held nine wagons and served Coldharbour Mill owned by the Fox Brothers of Wellington. It was a large worsted woollen mill and had a steam engine to supplement the water wheel. Coal for the steam engine was brought to the public siding. This siding was inspected and passed by Major General Hutchinson on 19th May, 1877 and opened the following month. Messrs Fox paid for signalling equipment at this siding. Thomas Fox had invested £2,000 in ordinary CVLR shares.

Because the Zulu and Boer wars had revealed that the scarlet uniform of the British army made those wearing it easy targets, in 1881 a Parliamentary Commission decided that the colour should be changed to khaki, this being a

View down, 28th August, 1953 showing Tiverton Junction after quadrupling.
Dr A.J.G. Dickens

Tiverton Junction, view up 16th June, 1986 shortly after closure to passengers on 12th May.
Author

DESCRIPTION OF THE LINE 53

Signalman Ken Snell looks out of Tiverton Junction box, 22nd July, 1972.   *Col M.H. Cobb*

Signalman Michael Mears in Tiverton Junction box, 4th July, 1977.   *Col M.H. Cobb*

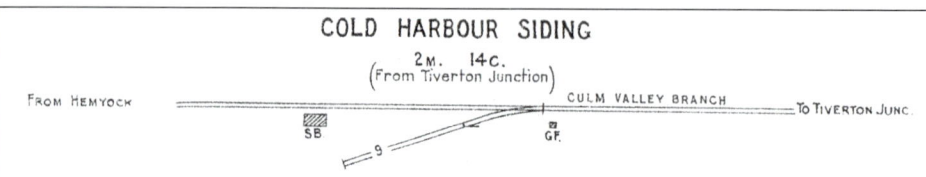

Plan of Cold Harbour c.1925. A digit indicates the number of wagons the siding could hold.

Coldharbour Halt view down on 8th June, 1963. A short length of the siding may be seen on the far left beyond the branch line. The posts have had the lamp casing, complete with oil reservoir and glass funnel, removed. *Author*

'14XX' class 0-4-2T No. 1450 and ex-LMS and ex-GWR Taunton RU (restricted use) brake vans at Coldharbour Halt with Coldharbour Mill in the background. *David Lawrence*

camouflage shade. Fox Brothers obtained the contract for making 5,000 puttees in the new colour. Although as Quakers they were opposed to war, they realised that the new colour would save lives, so accepted the contract. This also had the benefit of creating local employment, in fact spinning worsted yarn for puttees became a company speciality. When the mill closed in 1981, it became a working museum.

A short distance beyond the siding was Coldharbour Halt (2 m. 18 ch.). The GWR spelt it with both one and two words. The sleeper-edged platform, 50 ft (one coach) in length, surmounted by a timber shelter, opened on Saturday 23rd February, 1929. It served the hamlets of Smithincott and Stenhall as well as Coldharbour. The former was half a mile from Uffculme station, but only ¼ mile from the new halt, and Stenhall three miles from Tiverton Junction but only 1½ miles from the halt. Coldharbour had a population of 200, Smithincott 100 and Stenhall 80. At both Coldharbour and Whitehall halts the guard delivered the London papers, collecting the weekly payment from a tobacco tin located in the eaves of the waiting room shelter. Like all the branch platforms it was situated on the left side facing Hemyock. Coldharbour was the only station on the line with car parking facilities. It closed to passengers and goods on 9th September, 1963 and the site of the halt and siding is now a car park for the woollen museum.

Beyond the station the crossing keeper's hut doubled as a ticket office, a canopied window provided at its rear. It is believed that with the halt's opening, the GWR renewed Pain's original crossing hut. The keeper was not overworked: in 1935 an average of two carts used it daily. Beyond the erstwhile crossing, the trackbed to Uffculme is now a public footpath maintained by the Uffculme Trust and passes over a mill leat on a plate girder bridge.

Approaching Uffculme was a facing private siding. The agreement dated 9th October, 1919 was with W.J. Williams, slaughterer, and special trains brought hundreds of animals, mainly sheep, from all over the West of England. Carcasses in refrigerated meat vans were dispatched from the siding. About 1935 the mill was taken over by George Small & Sons Ltd and produced animal feed. The GWR made an agreement with him on 27th October, 1938. The ground frame was originally at 2 miles 55 chains, but in 1949 the siding was lengthened to 550 ft and the ground frame moved westwards to 2 miles 51 chains when the mill itself was extended. Cattle cake ingredients arrived by rail: grain in wagons and molasses in tanks.

Protecting the level crossing immediately before Uffculme station was the only home signal latterly on the branch and unusual in having no distant signal. The situation of this crossing, and also that at Culmstock, was inconvenient for road users as shunting held up traffic. New 20 ft-wide crossing gates were installed in February 1969 in connection with road widening required by Devon County Council, which paid for the work.

Uffculme station, 2 miles 62 chains, was on a sharp curve, the station building being of typical Pain design, brick-built with ornamental timber framing offering no structural benefit and over the years some fell away. The roof was pan-tiled and the station gas-lit. The 120 ft long platform had a well-maintained garden. The station closed to passengers on 9th September, 1960. Uffculme was the only station on the branch to have Great Western lamp tablets: one was displayed above the booking office door and the other on a lamp post.

THE CULM VALLEY LIGHT RAILWAY

Coldharbour Halt view down c.1960. Notice the timber waiting shelter, sleeper-faced platform, ugly concrete lamp post with 'Cold Harbour Halt' at the top of the glass. The crossing keeper's hut is beyond. In the foreground is a bridge over a stream. *Lens of Sutton*

The road side of the crossing keeper's hut, with the ticket hatch, *right*. Notice the rather crudely painted timetable board; the fence of sleepers; kissing gate and the chimney bracing.
Lens of Sutton

Brake van view of the gates being opened to road traffic, 31st August, 1965. *Michael Farr*

Coldharbour level crossing from the cab of class '25' No. D7506, 22nd July, 1972, which was hauling 10 empty milk tanks. The 2¼ milepost can be seen in the middle distance. Note the check rail on the curve. *Col M.H. Cobb*

View west from Uffculme station, 28th August, 1953. Notice the gas lamp, complete with station nameplate, to the left of the nameboard. *Dr A.J.G. Dickens*

'14XX' class 0-4-2T No. 1450 with a down train approaching Uffculme c.1955. The headlamps indicate that the train is composed entirely of vehicles conforming to coaching stock requirements. Note the milepost indicating ¾ mile, whereas the true mileage was 2¾ miles. The buffer plank is supported by posts of two rails bolted together. *David Lawrence*

DESCRIPTION OF THE LINE

A goods loop passed through the 29 ft-long timber-built goods shed. Contemporary with the shed's door widening, a small, lean-to stone shed was added against a wall. A stub siding near the west end of the loop served cattle pens. The loop was worked by the Middle ground frame (2 m. 60 ch.) and the East ground frame (2 m. 65 ch.). In 1926 the goods shed was removed to allow the loop to be used for run-round purposes and a corrugated iron lock-up placed on the passenger platform east of the brick building. The one ton crane which had been in the goods shed was replaced around 1930 by a three ton crane in the yard. There were two further sidings, one having an end-loading dock. Uffculme was the principal station on the branch and, in addition to facilities for ordinary passenger and goods traffic, had a carriage dock. The South of England Hide & Skin Co. dispatched, in unsheeted open wagons, hides which had been covered with salt. It was permissible to propel empty coaching stock to Tiverton Junction.

Coal arrived for the gas works in the Leat and for the steam brewery; also coal for heating most homes and larger houses bought it more economically by a wagon load. The gas works was a two-man affair, one man and his assistant, in addition to maintaining the supply, dug up the road and laid supply pipes, connected new users and turned the street lights on and off. The employees of William Furze's brewery enjoyed a railway trip to Torquay on 16th August, 1879. For Levy Jones it was particularly memorable. Being late for the return train he ran, fell, broke a leg and dislocated his ankle.

Uffculme closed to goods 8th May, 1967, except for the private siding traffic, and the sidings were removed shortly afterwards. The site is now built on.

Immediately east of the station the line crossed the River Culm for the first time. The initial six-span timber bridge was replaced in 1914 by a single-span iron girder structure. In August 1970 it was believed that the Barlow rails on the underside of this bridge, and also a similar one at 4 miles 21 chains, were thought to be in a dangerous condition, but when the bridges were opened up for inspection, they were found in better condition than anticipated and it was agreed that reconstruction could be deferred for at least five years.

The line climbed at 1 in 216, steepening to 1 in 68 for 21 chains. Initially Ratsash Lane was crossed at Five Fords Crossing, a keeper's hut being provided, but later dispensed with due to the crossing falling into disuse. Latterly it was used as a lengthman's hut. The line descended at 1 in 1736/216 for ½ mile before rising at 1 in 168 to cross the Culm at 4 miles 21 chains by a three-span plate girder bridge. When it was installed in the early 1920s, two divers worked replacing the old pile bridge.

The gradient steepened to ½ mile of 1 in 154 to Culmstock (4 m. 79 ch.) where immediately before the station was a level crossing. The 120 ft-long platform was on a curve and the nameboard of enamel, with white letters on a blue background. A looped siding identical to that at Uffculme passed through the timber-built goods shed containing a one ton crane. This was removed in 1932 and replaced by a corrugated iron lock-up on the passenger platform. The station was lit by oil lamps. A stub siding served the cattle dock, while another siding ran to the other side of the cattle pen to a loading dock. In 1877 the yard had a 1½ ton crane, but by 1904 a one ton crane was in use. By 1938 a three ton crane was provided but removed by 1956. The West ground frame was at 4 miles 76 chains and the East at 5 miles 3 chains. The station became an unstaffed halt on 2nd May,

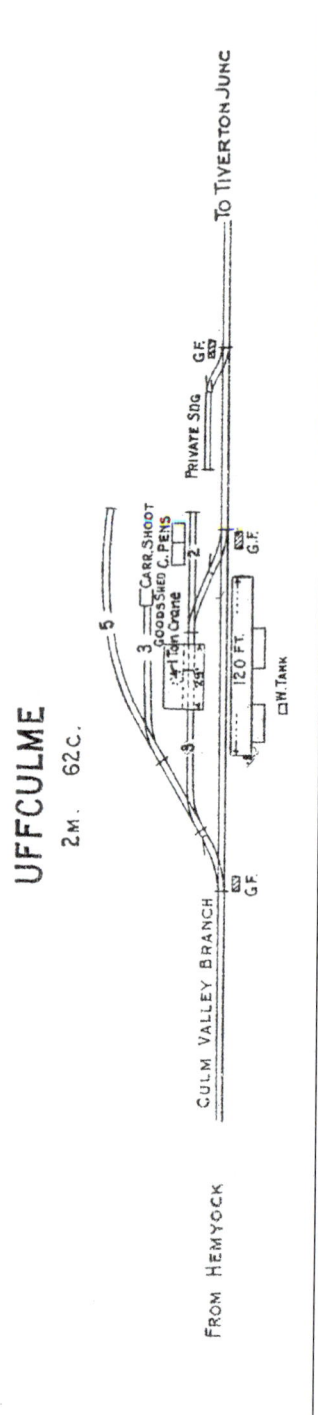

Above: Plan of Uffculme station c.1925. A digit indicates the number of wagons the siding could hold.

Above: Uffculme lamp tablet.

Right: The station nameboard preserved in Tiverton Museum. It is constructed of wood with timber lettering.
Author

DESCRIPTION OF THE LINE

'14XX' class 0-4-2T No. 1450 at Uffculme with a freight train. Notice the ex-LMS brake van behind the engine; the cattle dock, *left*; the station wheelbarrow by the goods shed door and a 40 gallon drum of paraffin for the level crossing gate lamps.
David Lawrence

'48XX' class 0-4-2T No. 4827 (later renumbered 1427) at Uffculme with an up train *c*.1947. The sheet-covered open wagon on the right still had 'GW' in large letters. A tube wagon is between the two other open wagons.
Lens of Sutton

Uffculme, view down, 8th June, 1963.   *Author*

Uffculme station, 9th May 1967. Some of the decorative wooden framework has been removed. A loud-sounding bell is still *in situ* on the front wall. Notice that the platform has been raised in front of the goods shed. This work was carried out in 1926. On the left edge of the picture is a telephone post with an enamel notice: 'You may telephone from here'.

A.E. West/South Western Circle

DESCRIPTION OF THE LINE

No. 1450 and an ex-LMS 20 ton and ex-GWR 'XP' 'Taunton RU' brake vans leaving Uffculme. On the right is Bridge No. 10 over the River Culm. Originally a seven-span timber viaduct, it was reconstructed in 1918 with two steel spans. *David Lawrence*

An up train at Five Fords Crossing, 24th August, 1950. In front of the ex-Barry Railway coach is an SR PMV (parcels and miscellaneous van). *R.J. Sellick*

CULMSTOCK
4M. 79C.

Plan of Culmstock station c.1925. A digit indicates the number of wagons the siding could hold.

Culmstock, view up c.1947. Some of the wooden decoration has been removed from the end wall. A sign between the corrugated iron goods shed and the station building carries the word 'Gentlemen'. Milepost 5 is on the left.

M.E.J. Deane courtesy Ian Bennett

DESCRIPTION OF THE LINE 65

The west end of Culmstock platform c.1947 with an Austin 16 car beyond.   *Author's Collection*

Culmstock, view east c.1947. The poster on the end of the building advertises Penzance as a holiday resort.   *M.E.J. Deane courtesy Ian Bennett*

No. 1421 with an ex-Eastern Region coach arrives at Culmstock with the 2.45 pm ex-Hemyock, 8th June, 1963. *Author*

Culmstock, view down 28th August, 1953. Notice the garden. *Dr A.J.G. Dickens*

DESCRIPTION OF THE LINE

1960. It closed to both passengers and goods on 9th September, 1963 and the ground frames and sidings were taken out of use on 28th October, 1963. The site is now part of the Culm Valley Inn (formerly the Railway Hotel) car park. Culmstock Mill, built as a woollen mill by Fox Brothers in the 1870s and later occupied by the Culm Valley Dairy Co., has been converted into dwellings.

The inhabitants of Culmstock are unkindly known to their neighbours as 'Culmstock baas' as a rebuke for having nurtured the last man to be hanged in England for sheep-stealing.

The line climbed at 1 in 94 for ¼ mile and ½ mile east of Culmstock crosses a 40-ft span girder bridge which replaced a timber bridge in 1922. A lane crossed at 6 miles 31 chains and the line reached Whitehall Halt (6 m. 33 ch.). The three wagon-long siding (6 m. 34 ch.), immediately beyond the passenger platform, predated the halt as it was opened at the commencement of the line. Although early attempts were made for Whitehall to deal with passengers, this did not come to pass until 27th February, 1933. Its construction was similar to that at Coldharbour, but the platform was even shorter and the waiting shelter sited between the wicket gate and the platform. The crossing keeper's hut stood on the opposite side of the line; the platform still remains. Locomotives were prohibited from running into the trailing siding. It was taken out of use on 28th October, 1963, the halt having closed on 9th September, 1963.

The line climbed for 22 chains at 1 in 76 and about midway to Hemyock at 6 miles 69 chains, a trailing siding, inspected by Major General Hutchinson on 19th May, 1877, led to Culm Davy Brickworks, crossing the Whitehall to Millhayes lane *en route*.

The line continued to climb and traversed a curve with a radius of 4¾ chains to the terminus at Hemyock, 7 miles 27 chains, about 400 ft above sea level and 168 ft higher than Tiverton Junction. Although named 'Hemyock', the village of that name was ½ mile distant, the station actually being in Millhayes.

The passenger station building was similar to the other two, but slightly larger measuring 50 ft by 12 ft by 15 ft. Over the years it received minor modifications, doors replacing windows and vice versa. In the 1920s a flat-roofed concrete block extension was built at the east end, the style clashing with that of Pain's design. The building contained Pooley 112 lb. scales and a Chubb safe. The platform measured 110 ft by 8 ft/6 ft (tapering) and 3 ft 6 in. in height. When a lengthy train prevented part of a coach from standing at the platform, portable wooden steps gave easy access. No drinking water was provided at the station, so staff filled a kettle at the dairy. The signal box at the west end of the passenger platform was reduced to a ground frame *circa* September 1925.

The station site was cramped and led to unusual track conformation. The run-round loop was immediately before the passenger platform, so this meant that trains had to reverse into the yard before a locomotive could run round. The goods shed, with a one ton crane by 1904, was at the rear of the passenger station and a siding trailed to the timber-built carriage shed, while a siding trailed off the run-round loop to the engine shed. By 1938 the yard had a three ton crane. A coaling stage and water tank were adjacent. Shortly after the line opened in 1876, a cattle dock was provided on the opposite side east of the passenger platform while the goods shed road was extended over a crossing to Millhayes Mill. This level crossing was unprotected by gates and was not allowed to be crossed by a locomotives so sufficient wagons had to be coupled to reach into this siding.

'14XX' class 0-4-2T No. 1451 with an up train on 25th May, 1952 passes Culmstock level crossing and the Railway Hotel. The first vehicle is an SR PMV. *R.J. Sellick*

Culmstock level crossing; notice the bridge rail post *right*; Taunton concrete works posts and a kissing gate, 9th May, 1967. *A.E. West/South Western Circle*

DESCRIPTION OF THE LINE

An 0-4-2T approaches Whitehall Halt with an up train. Notice the siding curving sharply to the right.
M.E.J. Deane courtesy Ian Bennett

Whitehall level crossing and halt. Notice that the waiting shelter is at the foot of the ramp and that the crossing gate has a spring catch. A passenger has parked his bicycle on the platform.
Lens of Sutton

WHITEHALL SIDING.
6 M. 34 C.

Plan of Whitehall Siding c.1925. A digit indicates the number of wagons the siding could hold.

The timber-walled platform at Whitehall Halt. On the far right is Bridge No. 27, originally a three-span timber bridge reconstructed in 1921 with a single-span steel girder type. On the right is a pile of chippings for packing under sleepers.

Lens of Sutton

DESCRIPTION OF THE LINE 71

On 28th October, 1975 class '25' diesel No. 25215 and a down train of empty milk tanks stops for the Whitehall level crossing gates to be opened by the guard. *Col M.H. Cobb*

Whitehall Halt from the verandah of a brake van on 31st August, 1965. The siding, formerly centre left, was taken out of use on 28th October, 1963 and subsequently lifted. *Michael Farr*

The rural situation of Hemyock goods yard; a 0-4-2T reverses from the passenger platform with an ex-Barry Railway coach, two fuel tanks and an ex-GWR brake van. The goods shed and crane stand on the right.
Colin Roberts Collection

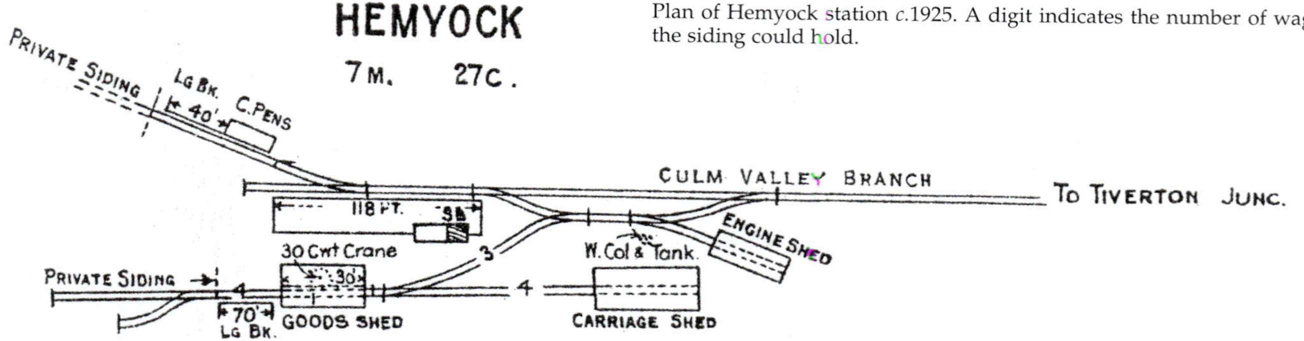

Plan of Hemyock station c.1925. A digit indicates the number of wagons the siding could hold.

DESCRIPTION OF THE LINE 73

General view of Hemyock goods yard looking towards the buffers. The former refreshment room can be seen above the open wagon and milk tank.   *M.E.J. Deane courtesy Ian Bennett*

Hemyock: goods shed and 3-ton crane *c*.1950.   *M.E.J. Deane courtesy Ian Bennett*

An SR PMV is being loaded from a Wilts United Dairy Co. lorry, 25th May, 1952. No. 1451 stands on original flat-bottomed rail. *R.J. Sellick*

'14XX' class 0-4-2T No. 1468 on an up mixed train, 21st September, 1959. *Michael Farr*

The water tank c.1949. Notice the 'devil' to prevent frost damage; also the soakaway. Portable steps on the left are for use with long trains. *M.E.J. Deane courtesy Ian Bennett*

No. 1451 arriving from Tiverton Junction with the 8.45 am, 6th November, 1962. *E.T. Gill*

An ex-Eastern Region coach at Hemyock, 8th June, 1963. No. 1421 had worked it as the 1.42 pm ex-Tiverton Junction. *Author*

The view to the milk factory, 21st September, 1959.   *Michael Farr*

Hemyock view east, 28th August, 1953, with Hemyock East ground frame (the former signal box) beyond the nameboard.   *Dr A.J.G. Dickens*

The station drive *right*, the kissing gate in the foreground and an 0-4-2T arriving with five wagons and an ex-GWR brake van. *M.E.J. Deane courtesy Ian Bennett*

View towards Tiverton Junction, 8th June, 1963. 'Patrol Post' on the gate perhaps indicates a Civil Defence exercise. *Author*

DESCRIPTION OF THE LINE

No. 1451 arrives at Hemyock with an ex-Barry Railway coach, four box vans and an ex-GWR brake van. The renewed cattle dock is on the left and catch points for potential runaways from the milk depot siding, can be seen in the centre of the picture. *Lens of Sutton*

Detail of the cattle dock at Hemyock. *A.E. West/South Western Circle*

Empty milk tanks being hauled across the road protected by a Unigate employee holding a 'Stop' sign.
Col M.H. Cobb

Shunting with tank wagons across the road at Hemyock, 30th September, 1973.   *Peter Triggs*

DESCRIPTION OF THE LINE

By an agreement of 17th July, 1920 with the Culm Valley Dairy Co., the cattle pen siding was extended across the road, the GWR paying £355 10s. 0d. which was half the cost. Laying this siding entailed slightly shortening the east end of the platform to form a terminal stub. A locomotive was permitted to pass over this gated crossing. Latterly keys to the gate were held by the milk factory staff who were also responsible for protecting both crossings. The crossings could only be used during the hours of daylight. Athough latterly milk tank wagons were winched to the dairy by factory staff, in practice this rarely happened due to the risk of breaking a wrist when winding a rope around the capstan. Normally sufficient wagons were placed in front of the locomotive to enable it to push tank wagons to the creamery without passing over the level crossing. Loaded tankers were returned by gravity, the road being protected by two flagmen. A porter from Hemyock station was given notice that the procedure was imminent, the announcement usually made by banging a spanner on a buffer. Wheel stops were fixed to the station side of both crossings and the keys held at the station. Coal for the dairy was unloaded by hand until after World War II when a conveyor was installed so subsequent deliveries were made in wagons with bottom door discharge. The siding also received empty tins to be filled with powdered milk.

In the early 1930s the goods yard layout was drastically altered. The engine shed closed on 21st October, 1929, while the carriage shed had fallen out of use. These were removed and the space used for a longer run-round loop, while on the north side of the running line a new looped siding served an asbestos-roofed corrugated iron goods shed standing on a timber platform. This replaced the original goods shed. The replacement shed is now in a field near Ashculme. Hemyock West ground frame (7 m. 17 ch.) was opened at the west end of the run-round loop and Hemyock East (7 m. 27 ch.) was the old signal box. Hemyock closed to passengers on 9th September, 1963 and to goods (excluding the milk traffic) on 6th September, 1965.

Closely adjoining the station on its north side, but not on railway property, in 1878 Richard Hine erected a refreshment room 55 ft by 17 ft accommodating 120 to 130 visitors. The 1877 summer had brought large numbers of trippers to the line and it was hoped that this facility would encourage even greater numbers. Unfortunately the anticipated army of visitors failed to appear so the refreshment rooms soon closed and were used for housing animals.

GWR paste pot and poster brush from Hemyock.

Traffic dealt with at branch stations 1903 to 1933.

Chapter Six

Events Leading to Closure

In the mid-1920s the GWR investigated the economics of various branch lines and found in 1925 that the Culm Valley receipts of £22,609 were only offset by costs of £5,901.*

	Paybill	
	1924	1925
	£	£
Uffculme	586	653
Culmstock	349	363
Hemyock	909	940
	1,844	1,956

A report of 24th February, 1926 recommended replacing passenger trains by road services, creating an annual saving of £810, and moving goods and milk traffic within an eight hour working day. This economy would have allowed engine and carriage sheds to be closed, the station master withdrawn from Culmstock and a reduction made in branch staff.

Expenses 1925

	£
Locomotive	3,133
Engineering dept	2,240
Signalling dept	233
Clothing	44
Fuel, light, water	49
Rates	202
	5,901

Average Number of Wagons Daily 1925

	Received	Forwarded
Coal and minerals	1	0
General goods	11	7

Statistics for 1925

2,866 cans of milk
1,185 trucks of livestock by goods
Coal consumption: coaching 20.4 lb./mile
                     freight 20.4 lb./mile
Five trips each way (four mixed)

In 1934 livestock traffic dived to 351 wagons annually. The following year, George Small built his grain mill at Uffculme on the site of the slaughterhouse and this brought new traffic to the line. The axle loading on the branch was raised to 13 tons 18 cwt and loaded 'Grano' hopper wagons were permitted to run as far as Small's private siding. Some wagons were branded to work between Avonmouth and Uffculme.

* Some of the official figures from RAIL 253/158 detailed on page 83 are at variance with those in RAIL 266/44 on page 82, both sourced from the National Archives, Kew.

CULM VALLEY BRANCH.

Single Line worked by Train Staff and only one Engine in Steam at a time. The Train Staff Stations are Tiverton Junction and Hemyock.

DOWN TRAINS.

M.P. Mileage.		STATIONS.	Ruling Gradient.	WEEK DAYS. K		B		B		B		B		B		B		B			SUNDAYS. D			
				Goods. §		Mixed.		Mixed. SX		Pass. SO		Mixed.		Passenger. R		Mixed. Y		Passenger. SO			Engine and Van.			
M.	C.			arr.	dep.	arr.	dep.	arr.	dep.	arr.	dep.	arr.	dep.	arr.	dep.	arr.	dep.	arr.	dep.		arr.	dep.		
				a.m.	a.m.	a.m.	a.m.	a.m.	a.m.	a.m.	a.m.	p.m.	p.m.	p.m.	p.m.	p.m.	p.m.	p.m.	p.m.		p.m.	p.m.		
—	—	**TIVERTON JUNCTION**	—	—	**5 50**	—	**8 45**	—	**11 30**	—	*11 30*	—	**12 50**	—	**4‡30**	—	**7 0**	—	*9 10*	..	—	*7† 0*	..	..
2	20	Coldharbour Halt	67 R.	—	—	8 53½	8 54½	1138½	1139½	*1138½*	*1139½*	1258½	1259½	4‡38½	4‡39½	7 8½	7 9½	*9 18½*	*9 19½*	....	—	—	....	....
2	68	Uffculme	150 R.	6 1	6 22	8 57	9 12	11 42	—	*11 42*	*11 50*	1 2	1 8	4‡42	4‡47	7 12	7 17	*9 22*	*9 23*	..	**R**	**R**	..	..
5	5	Culmstock	68 R.	6 31	6 41	9 21	9 30	▬	▬	*12 0*	—	1 17	1 23	4‡56	4‡57	7 26	7 27	*9 32*	*9 33*	....	—	—	....	....
6	40	Whitehall Halt	94 R.	**C**	**R**	9 36½	9 37½	..	..	▬	▬	1 30½	1 33½	5‡3½	5‡4½	7 33½	7 34½	*9 41½*	*9 43½*	..	—	—	..	..
7	33	**HEMYOCK**	76 R.	**7 0**	—	**9 42**	—	....	....	....	....	**1 38**	—	**5‡ 9**	—	**7 39**	—	*9 48*	—	....	*1†45*	—	....	....

UP TRAINS.

STATIONS.	Ruling Gradient.			WEEK DAYS. B		B		B		B		B		B		B		B		SUNDAYS. C			
				Passenger.		Passenger.		Mixed. SX		Passenger. SO		Mixed.		Passenger.		Mixed. Z		Passenger. SO		Milk. RR			
				arr.	dep.	arr.	dep.	arr.	dep.	arr.	dep.	arr.	dep.	arr.	dep.	arr.	dep.	arr.	dep.	arr.	dep.		
				a.m.	a.m.	a.m.	a.m.	p.m.	p.m.	p.m.	p.m.	p.m.	p.m.	p.m.	p.m.	p.m.	p.m.	p.m.	p.m.	p.m.	p.m.		
HEMYOCK	—	..	..	—	**7 30**	—	**10 30**	..	..	..	..	—	**2 35**	—	**5 50**	—	**8 5**	—	*10 0*	—	*2 20*	..	..
Whitehall Halt	76 F.	....	....	7 34½	7 35½	1034½	1035½	....	....	....	....	2 39½	2 40½	5 54½	5 55½	8 9½	8 10½	*10 4½*	*10 6½*	—	—	....	....
Culmstock	94 F.	..	..	7 42	7 43	10 42	10 44	..	**V**	—	*12 5*	2 47	2 55	6 2	6 4	8 20	8 21	*10 15*	*10 16*	—	—	..	..
Uffculme	68 F.	....	....	7 52	7 53	10 53	10 54	—	12 10	*12 14*	*12 15*	3 4	3 11	6 13	6 14	8 30	8 31	*10 25*	*10 26*	—	—	....	....
Coldharbour Halt	150 F.	..	..	7 55½	7 56½	1056½	1057½	1212½	1219½	*1217½*	*1219½*	3 13½	3 14½	6 16½	6 17½	8 33½	8 34½	—	—	—	—	..	..
Stopboard 0m. 23½c.	—	....	....	—	**P**	—	**P**	—	**P**	—	**P**	—	**P**	—	**P**	—	**P**	—	**P**	—	—	....	....
TIVERTON JUNCTION	67 F.	..	..	**8 5**	—	**11 7**	—	**12 28**	—	*12 28*	—	**3 25**	—	**6 28**	—	**8 43**	—	*10 40*	—	*3 5*	—	..	..

The Branch is worked between Tiverton Junction and Hemyock stations by means of one engine in steam carrying a staff. The speed of trains must not exceed fifteen miles per hour on any part of the Branch The Locomotive Engines, Carriages, and Vehicles used must not have a greater weight than thirteen tons eighteen cwts. on any one pair of wheels. Special 8-wheel Passenger Coaches are provided to work on the Branch. Ordinary 8-wheel stock for passenger use, vehicles over 60-ft. in length, and also 6-wheel Stock (with the exception of 6-wheel Milk Tanks) are prohibited. The Branch is worked by engines of the 0-4-2 Tank type. The engine is prohibited from using :—

Uffculme.—Loading Bank Siding, and Small's Siding. **Whitehall.**—Siding. **Culmstock.**—Loading Bank—not to approach within thirty yards of dead end.
The G.W. Standard Load Gauge applies over the Branch. **Hemyock.**—Private Siding not protected by Level Crossing Gates.

Long Round Timber.—Long Round Timber must not be accepted for transit at Uffculme, Culmstock, or Hemyock

R—To convey Meat Vans for Uffculme. **V**—Not to convey wagons from Uffculme for Tiverton Junction. **Y**—Wagons not to be detached or attached at Culmstock and not to convey more than two wagons for Hemyock. To convey cattle traffic for Uffculme as necessary. **Z**—Will convey goods wagons from Hemyock only. ‡—To run 5 minutes later on Saturdays. §—Runs as a Mixed Train, Uffculme to Culmstock.

Trainmen to open and close Crossing Gates as shown below :—

- 5.50 a.m. Tiverton Junction to Hemyock—Cold Harbour and Uffculme
- 7. 0 p.m. Tiverton Junction to Hemyock—Whitehall
- 9.10 p.m. Tiverton Junction to Hemyock **SO**—Whitehall
- 5.50 p.m. Hemyock to Tiverton Junction—Whitehall
- 8. 5 p.m. Hemyock to Tiverton Junction—Whitehall
- 10. 0 p.m. Hemyock to Tiverton Junction **SO**—Whitehall and Cold Harbour

} Fireman to open gates on arrival of train, and guard to close gates across the line after train has drawn clear of crossings.

Working timetable 3rd July, 1939 to 24th September, 1939.

EVENTS LEADING TO CLOSURE

An up train arrives at Culmstock c.1947. Coach No. 2312 is in wartime brown livery. C. Small & Sons cart, shaftless, is used as a platform to enable full sacks to be moved directly to the lorry.
M.E.J. Deane courtesy Ian Bennett

'14XX' class 0-4-2T No. 1449 at Uffculme with a down train c.1950. Note the severe curve. The 3-ton crane and goods yard stand to the left of the ex-Barry Railway coach and above it can be seen George Small's mill. The guard is leaning out of the second coach, separated from the other by an open wagon.
B.L. Jackson

CULM VALLEY BRANCH.

Single Line worked by Train Staff and only one Engine in Steam at a time. The Train Staff Stations are Tiverton Junction and Hemyock.

DOWN TRAINS.

WEEK DAYS. | SUNDAYS.

M.P. Mileage. M.	C.	STATIONS.	Ruling Gradient.	K Freight.§ arr.	dep.	B Mixed. arr.	dep.	B Mixed. SX arr.	dep.	B Pass. SO arr.	dep.	B Mixed arr.	dep.	B Passenger. arr.	dep.	B Mixed. Y arr.	dep.				D Milk. Empties. arr.	dep.		
				a.m.	a.m.	a.m.	a.m.	a.m.	a.m.	a.m.	a.m.	p.m.	p.m.	p.m.	p.m.	p.m.	p.m.				a.m.	a.m.		
—	—	**TIVERTON JUNCTION**	—	—	**5 50**	—	**8 45**	—	**11 35**	—	*11 35*	—	**1 30**	—	**4 33**	—	**7 10**	..	..	..	—	**8†15**	..	..
2	20	Coldharbour Halt	67 R.	—	—	8 53½	8 54½	1143½	1144½	*1143½*	*1144½*	1 38½	1 39½	4 41½	4 42	7 18½	7 19½	....	....	....	—	—	....	....
2	68	Uffculme	150 R.	**6 1**	**6 22**	8 57	9 12	11 47	—	*11 47*	*12 0*	1 42	1 43	4 45	4 46	7 22	7 27	..	..	..	—	—	..	..
5	5	Culmstock	68 R.	**6 31**	**6 41**	9 21	9 30	▬	▬	*12 5*	—	1 54	1 55	4 55	4 56	7 36	7 37	....	....	....	—	—	....	....
6	40	Whitehall Halt	94 R.	**C**	**R**	9 36½	9 37½	..	..	▬	▬	2 3½	2 4½	5 2½	5 3½	7 43½	7 44½	..	..	..	—	—	..	..
7	33	**HEMYOCK**	76 R.	**7 0**	—	**9 42**	—	....	....	....	....	**2 10**	—	**5 8**	—	**7 49**	—	....	....	....	**9† 0**	—	....	....

UP TRAINS.

WEEK DAYS. | SUNDAYS.

STATIONS.	Ruling Gradient.			B Passenger. arr.	dep.	B Passenger. arr.	dep.	B Mixed. SX arr.	dep.	B Passenger. SO arr.	dep.	B Mixed. arr.	dep.	B Mixed. arr.	dep.	B Mixed. Z arr.	dep.			C Milk. arr.	dep.		
				a.m.	a.m.	a.m.	a.m.	p.m.	p.m.	p.m.	p.m.	p.m.	p.m.	p.m.	p.m.	p.m.	p.m.			p.m.	p.m.		
HEMYOCK	—	..	..	—	**7 30**	—	**10 30**	..	..	..	..	—	**3 0**	—	**5 55**	—	**8 8**	..	..	—	**3 40**	..	..
Whitehall Halt	76 F.	....	....	7 34½	7 35	1034½	1035½	....	....	....	....	3 5	3 6	5 59½	6 0½	8 12½	8 13	....	....	—	—	....	....
Culmstock	94 F.	..	..	7 41½	7 42	10 42	10 44	..	**V**	—	*12 10*	3 13	3 15	6 7	6 9	8 19½	8 20½	..	..	—	—	..	..
Uffculme	68 F.	....	....	7 50	7 51	10 53	10 54	—	12 10	*12 19*	*12 20*	3 24	3 27	6 18	6 19	8 29½	8 30½	....	....	—	—	....	....
Coldharbour Halt	150 F.	..	..	7 53½	7 54	1056½	1057½	1212½	1219½	*1222½*	*1224½*	3 30	3 31	6 21½	6 22½	8 33	8 33½	..	..	—	—	..	..
Stopboard 0m. 23½c.	—	....	....	—	**P**	—	**P**	—	**P**	—	**P**	—	**P**	—	**P**	—	**P**	....	....	—	**P**	....	....
TIVERTON JUNCTION	67 F.	..	..	**8 2**	—	**11 7**	—	**12 28**	—	*12 33*	—	**3 41**	—	**6 33**	—	**8 42**	—	..	..	**4 25**	—	..	..

The Branch is worked between Tiverton Junction and Hemyock stations by means of one engine in steam carrying a staff. The speed of trains must not exceed fifteen miles per hour on any part of the Branch. The Locomotive Engines, Carriages, and Vehicles used must not have a greater weight than thirteen tons eighteen cwts. on any one pair of wheels. Special 8-wheel Passenger Coaches are provided to work on the Branch. Ordinary 8-wheel stock for passenger use, vehicles over 60-ft. in length, and also 6-wheel Stock (with the exception of 6-wheel Milk Tanks) are prohibited. The Branch is worked by engines of the 0–4–2 Tank type. The engine is prohibited from using :—

Uffculme.—Loading Bank Siding, and Small's Siding. **Whitehall.**—Siding. **Culmstock.**—Loading Bank—not to approach within thirty yards of dead end.
The G.W. Standard Load Gauge applies over the Branch. **Hemyock.**—Private Siding not protected by Level Crossing Gates.

Long Round Timber.—Long Round Timber must not be accepted for transit at Uffculme, Culmstock, or Hemyock.

V—Not to convey wagons from Uffculme for Tiverton Junction. **Y**—Wagons not to be detached or attached at Culmstock and not to convey more than two wagons for Hemyock. To convey cattle traffic for Uffculme as necessary. **Z**—Will convey goods wagons from Hemyock only. §—Runs as a Mixed Train, Uffculme to Culmstock.

Trainmen to open and close Crossing Gates as shown below :—

5.50 a.m. Tiverton Junction to Hemyock—Cold Harbour and Uffculme
7.10 p.m. Tiverton Junction to Hemyock—Whitehall
5.55 p.m. Hemyock to Tiverton Junction—Whitehall
8. 8 p.m. Hemyock to Tiverton Junction—Whitehall

} Fireman to open gates on arrival of train, and guard to close gates across the line after train has drawn clear of crossings.

Working timetable summer 1947.

EVENTS LEADING TO CLOSURE

Goods traffic peaked in 1938 at 26,345 tons and declined to about half this figure in the 1960s. From 1939 livestock traffic comprised only one or two wagons weekly. The April 1951 *Railway Observer* commented:

The passenger service is only kept going by reason of the fact that the profitable milk trains from Hemyock must be braked officially by passenger-carrying vehicles, though on several occasions recently a freight 4-wheel brake van has been up the branch.

About 1955 much of the branch track was renewed and oil from Avonmouth had replaced coal as fuel for the milk factory. At this period trains averaged five passengers. On 2nd May, 1960, as an economy measure Culmstock was unstaffed and became a halt. Another economy was the withdrawal of gatekeepers from July 1960 so, from then on, trainmen were required to operate the gates. The keys were kept in Tiverton Junction signal box and the fireman obtained two keys and handed one to the guard. The fireman was responsible for returning both keys to the signalman on arrival back at Tiverton Junction. By 1962 the Uffculme station master was also in charge of Hemyock. Passenger receipts for 1962 were less than £1,000 per annum, yet the expense of working the service was £2,489.

The last passenger train ran on Saturday 7th September, 1963. Both coaches were used and accommodation was increased by placing benches from Tiverton Junction's down side waiting room in one of the guard's vans. In addition to the normal services, an extra was put on, primarily for the benefit of Hemyock residents to enable them to have a last trip on the line. This left Tiverton Junction at 3.35 pm, arrived at Hemyock 4.13, departed 4.20 and arrived Tiverton Junction at 4.58. On this final day of passenger services, a coal wagon was seen at Uffculme and three open wagons at Uffculme mill. Except at Hemyock, very little local interest was shown in the closure and, following the withdrawal of the service, no additional buses were run.

Almost 100 passengers were carried on the very last train which also had two milk tanks. 0-4-2T No. 1421 was specially cleaned for the occasion and its crew consisted of driver J. Fewings and fireman E. Laskey. Culmstock and Coldharbour Siding closed to goods from 9th September, 1963.

On Monday 9th September, 1963 No. D2140, a 204 bhp diesel-mechanical 0-6-0 worked the goods and apart from a few occasions when a diesel was unavailable, such as 21st December, 1963 when 0-4-2T No. 1450 was used, steam locomotives no longer appeared. The timetable from 9th September was: Tiverton Junction depart 6.45 am, return 8.45 am from Hemyock; return trip 11.25 am to Uffculme, extended to Hemyock if required; Tiverton Junction depart 3.20 pm to Hemyock, returning from Hemyock at 4.30 pm. On Sundays the train left Tiverton Junction at 2.00 pm and left Hemyock at 3.30 pm.

Supplementary Operating Instructions dated September 1964 stated that from October 1963 the branch was worked as siding under the supervision of the station master at Uffculme in conjunction with his colleague at Tiverton Junction. Except in an emergency there was to be only 'one engine in steam'; all points on the line were hand-operated; the time of departure from each of the three stations was to be advised to the station in advance by telephone; the speed limit was 15 mph. Engines and vehicles working over the line must not

Clerestory coach No. 2312 at Hemyock *c.*1949 in World War II brown livery. 'Culm Valley' is branded on the sole bar, '22' on its end is its weight in tons.   *M.E.J. Deane courtesy Ian Bennett*

The 3.00 pm to Tiverton Junction leaves Hemyock in October 1950. It consists of an ex-Barry Railway coach and seven milk tanks. The River Culm is on the left.
M.E.J. Deane courtesy Ian Bennett

George Small's siding, Uffculme, *left*, view up, 25th May, 1952, showing the severe curve. '14XX' class 0-4-2T No. 1451 has coach No. W263 with an ex-SR PMV next to the engine. *R.J. Sellick*

No. 1405 at Hemyock beside the River Culm. Note the erosion protection measures.
M.E.J. Deane courtesy Ian Bennett

No. 1420 about to depart with the 6.00 pm to Tiverton Junction, 15th July, 1960. *M.H. Walshaw*

'A4' class 4-6-2 No. 60022 *Mallard* with the up 'West Countryman' at Tiverton Junction 24th February, 1963. The petrol storage depot is beyond the engine. Enthusiasts appear not to consider safety.
Revd Alan Newman

'45XX' class 2-6-2T Nos. 4591 and 5564 arriving at Tiverton Junction, 24th February, 1963, with the 'West Countryman' special. The locomotive shed is on the far left.
Hugh Ballantyne

The Locomotive Club of Great Britain 'West Countryman' on 24th February, 1963 used '14XX' class 0-4-2T No. 1450 (83C Exeter), the two ex-Eastern Region coaches and five brake vans for the Hemyock branch part of the tour. Here it is standing at Tiverton Junction down main platform. Passengers returned to London hauled by No. 60022 *Mallard*. The '14XX' class engine at the other end of the train probably brought the brake vans from Exeter Riverside yard.

Hugh Ballantyne

The 6.00 pm Hemyock to Tiverton Junction about to leave Hemyock on 7th September, 1963. It was the last passenger train on the branch.   *Author's Collection*

EVENTS LEADING TO CLOSURE

Uffculme station and bridge from the cab of class '25' No. D7506 on 22nd July, 1965. The track has been relaid with flat-bottomed rail and the old chaired sleepers are on the left awaiting collection. The last of the 10 milk tanks has just crossed Bridge No. 10. Notice the close proximity of the fence to the track.
Col M.H. Cobb

Diesel-mechanical 204 bhp shunter No. D2175 near George Small's mill, 9th May, 1967, with a down goods comprising three Regent fuel tanks and at least two open wagons. The coach on the right is a Bedford.
A.E. West/South Western Circle

exceed a weight of 13 tons 18 cwt on any one pair of wheels except 36 tons gross class 'B' tank wagons which may work to Hemyock, and loaded 20 ton grain wagons may work between Tiverton Junction and the private siding at Uffculme. Vehicles over 60 ft in length and six-wheeled stock - except for milk tanks - were prohibited from working over the line. When a train was worked by a single-manned diesel locomotive the guard was responsible for obtaining the key and both opening and closing the crossing gates and returning the key to the signalman at Tiverton Junction.

Hemyock station was unstaffed from 1st October, 1970 and the station and platform demolished to improve visibility when shunting the milk sidings. By September the following year all the other station buildings on the branch had been demolished and only cut-back platform mounds remained. In 1972 new signs were erected at all crossings. With the construction of the M5 in the spring of 1975, a crossing called 'Motorway' at 0 miles 12 chains was installed between Tiverton Junction and the erstwhile Coldharbour Halt. Unigate, with 33 staff on its Hemyock payroll, dropped a bombshell when it announced that it was closing its factory on 31st October, 1975. Class '25' No. 25215 drew 14 milk tanks to Hemyock on 28th October and seven full tanks were taken away by No. 25063 on 31st October forming the very last train. Although BR printed tickets for this final run, safety regulations of the Department of the Environment prevented the trip from being operated with passengers, so the line closed without ceremony - it had missed its centenary by just seven months.

No. D2141 running around its train on 31st August, 1965. The brake van is branded 'Taunton RU'. *Michael Farr*

Class '25' No. D7577 shunting milk tanks at Hemyock prior to leaving with three full tanks, 4th January, 1972.
Col M.H. Cobb

An up milk train passes milepost 1 on 20th September, 1974. No. 25082 has three milk tanks, a box van and two brake vans containing Cambridge University Railway Club members.
Col M.H. Cobb

No. 25215 on 28th October, 1975 with 14 empty milk tanks on the newly-laid flat-bottomed track. Bridge No. 10 is on the far left. Notice the lack of earthworks. *Col M.H. Cobb*

Rear view of a train of 14 empty milk tanks, the final supply, leaving Tiverton Junction up the gradient of 1 in 66 behind No. 25215 on 28th October, 1975. The motorway works are beyond.
Col M.H. Cobb

EVENTS LEADING TO CLOSURE

No. 25063 crossing the 80 ft span Bridge No. 7 near Selgar's Mill. Originally a six-span timber viaduct, it was replaced in 1921 by this bowstring girder bridge. The engine is proceeding in a down direction and drew no empties as it was the last day of working the branch, 31st October, 1975. *Col W.H. Cobb*

The last train on the branch leaves Hemyock on 31st October, 1975. It comprises No. 25063 and seven milk tanks. *Col M.H. Cobb*

View 13th August, 1976 towards the main line at Tiverton Junction along the formation of the Hemyock branch. On the left is the stop block of the stub siding on which stands a tamper. The siding was eventually taken out of use *circa* March 1983. The fence borders the motorway.
Col M.H. Cobb

'Western' class diesel-hydraulic No. 1065 *Western Consort* at Tiverton Junction restarting a train of telegraph poles, 19th September, 1976 after a 'Stop and inspect'. The train had been collecting poles towards Whiteball tunnel. Returning, the jib of the crane, unfortunately left in the raised position, struck the bridge of the North Devon Link Road at Sampford Peverell and the crane was thrown off the 'Larmak' carrying it. The train was sent into the Hemyock branch platform for inspection. It consisted of six 'Prawns' with poles; one 'Larmak'; six open wagons and a brake van.
Col M.H. Cobb

Tiverton Junction view up 16th June, 1986 showing the Esso depot on the left and the stub of the Hemyock branch on the right. On the former branch a stop block has been erected at the end of the platform. *Author*

Crossways cutting, Willand, view towards Tiverton Junction, 25th August, 2004. *Author*

Bridge No. 9 on the walkway between Coldharbour and Uffculme, 21st June, 2004. Originally a two-span timber bridge, it was reconstructed in 1916 with a steel span. *Author*

The preserved Whitehall Halt, view towards Hemyock, 21st June, 2004. *Author*

EVENTS LEADING TO CLOSURE

The enamel Culmstock nameboard has reflected the light unlike the wooden nameboard below. The picture was taken in Tiverton Museum. *Author*

Branch Traffic for January to June 1975

	Inwards			Outwards		
	Wagons	Tonnes	Revenue £	Wagons	Tonnes	Revenue £
Uffculme (cattle feed)	70	840	-	3	30	56
Hemyock (milk)	-	-	-	172	2,401	9,635

As Uffculme traffic alone was insufficient to make the line economically viable, closure of the milk depot meant closure of the line.

Track recovery was deferred due to a dispute with the National Union of Railwaymen. This was settled in September 1976 and track lifting commenced at Hemyock on 16th December and by 23rd January, 1977 the track had been lifted as far as Culmstock, the rest of the branch was soon recovered. The estimated profit from closure (i.e. value of materials less cost of recovery) was £89,850 and the actual profit £93,715.09.

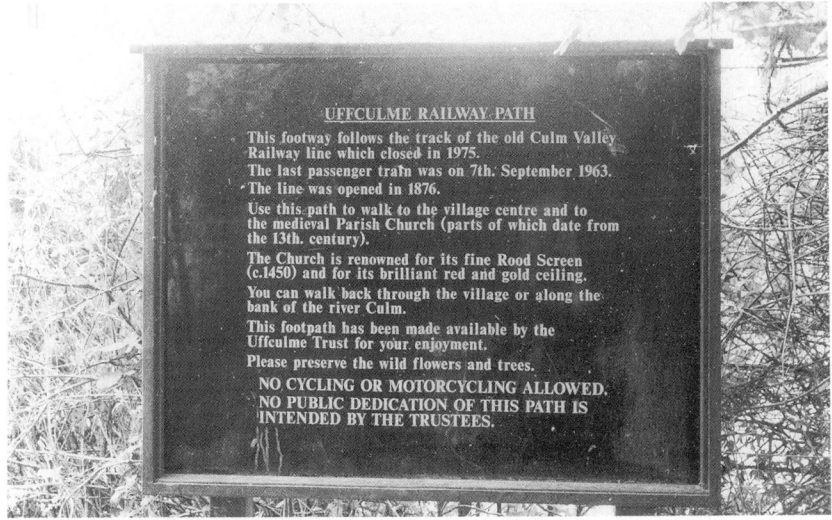

The Uffculme Railway Path notice, 21st June, 2004. *Author*

No. 1376 was formerly Bristol & Exeter Railway 0-6-0T No. 114 built in September 1874 for working the CVLR. In September 1881 it was rebuilt at Swindon with a longer wheelbase and a new boiler. No. 1376 was then sent to Weymouth where it spent most of its life. Here it is seen there c.1904, just inside the yard, with the Quay Tramway beyond. *M.J. Tozer Collection*

0-4-2T No. 1385 *John Owen*, originally an 0-6-0T, its rear coupling rods were removed converting it to an 0-4-2T to enable it to traverse the sharp curves of the CVLR more easily. It is shown here at Exeter, St David's. *Author's Collection*

Chapter Seven

Locomotives

The Bristol & Exeter Railway, being principally a broad gauge company, did not own any suitable standard gauge locomotives for working the CVLR, so James Pearson, B&E locomotive superintendent, designed two 0-6-0Ts specially for the line. Numbered 114 and 115, they were constructed in the B&E locomotive works at Bristol. The equally divided wheelbase was 10 ft 6 in., the wheels 3 ft 6 in. in diameter and the engine measured 21 ft in length over the buffers. Each locomotive weighed 20 tons 8 cwt and the cylinders were 12 in. by 18 in. Both engines were fitted with a marine-type water tube boiler, as opposed to the normal fire tube boiler. As the cylindrical firebox was enclosed within the boiler, this permitted a well-tank to be fitted between the frames to augment the small side tanks. Total water capacity was 320 gallons. The coal bunkers were in front of the cab and above the side tanks. The cab was of Manning, Wardle pattern. No. 114 was completed in September 1874 and No. 115 in December 1875. By the time the line opened on 29th May, 1876 the GWR had taken over the B&E and renumbered the engines Nos. 1376 and 1377.

In July 1876 when working the CVLR, one became derailed, so the following month GWR locomotive superintendent Joseph Armstrong instructed that the coupling rods be shortened to convert the engine to an 0-4-2T arrangement. From henceforth all subsequent steam engines used on the branch were four-coupled designs. Presumably these ex-B&E engines were not a success, as they were both rebuilt as 0-6-0Ts in September 1881 with an increased wheelbase of 6 ft 3 in. + 6 ft 3 in. and given new boilers with fire tubes. They were fitted with pillared cabs and sent to Weymouth for use on the Quay Tramway. No. 1377 was rebuilt again in January 1915 and eventually withdrawn in January 1927, the month its sister No. 1376 was transferred to Oswestry where she worked the Tanat Valley branch until withdrawal in January 1934.

Nos. 1376/7 were replaced on the CVLR by Nos. 1298 and 1300. These started life on the South Devon Railway (SDR) as two of a batch of three 2-4-0Ts. They were under construction at the company's works in Newton Abbot when the SDR was amalgamated with the GWR on 1st February, 1876. Construction of the first engine had started in June 1875 and on the other two the following month. The boilers, and most of the other items, had been purchased from the Ince Forge Co. Following the amalgamation, construction was transferred to Swindon and here they were finished as 2-4-0 side tank engines, all leaving the works in December 1878. They had a wheelbase of 5 ft 8 in. + 6 ft 4 in.; 4 ft diameter driving wheels; a water capacity of 324 gallons and with full tanks the locomotive weighed 22 tons 12 cwt. Nos. 1298 and 1300 took over Culm Valley working in 1881 and were generally based at Exeter or Hemyock in rotation. No. 1298 was withdrawn in October 1926 and No. 1300 in May 1934. The latter had been rebuilt in February 1905. No. 1299, made into a crane engine, never worked on the branch. '1298' class locomotives were restricted to the following number of vehicles on the branch: coal and mineral 4; goods 6; mixed 7; empties 8.

Although these two engines were the principal branch engines for over 40 years, others appeared. One such was ex-Whitland & Taf Vale Railway 0-6-0ST No. 1 *John*

2-4-0T No. 1300 outside Hemyock engine shed, 25th May, 1929, with the carriage shed and water tank *right*.
H.C. Casserley

2-4-0T No. 1300 which worked on the branch 1881-1934.
Amyas Crump Collection

2-4-0T No. 1300 which worked on the branch 1881-1934. *Amyas Crump Collection*

2-4-0T No. 1300. Its construction was started by the South Devon Railway but completed by the GWR in 1878. No. 1300 took over CVLR working in 1881. This photograph was taken in 1934 shortly before its withdrawal in May. *Colin Roberts Collection*

No. 1468 by the water tank at Hemyock, 21st September, 1959. *Michael Farr*

No. 1451 (83C Exeter), bearing the early BR crest, is beside coach No. W268 at Culmstock *c.*1951.
M.E.J. Deane courtesy Ian Bennett

Owen, Fox, Walker & Co. No. 170 of 1872. It was taken over by the GWR on 1st September, 1886 and renumbered 1385. For some years before rebuilding in July 1894 it worked as an 0-4-2T, so that it could negotiate the curves on the Culm Valley branch more easily. The GWR sold it out of service in August 1912 and it worked at Cornsay Colliery, Durham, before scrapping *circa* 1952.

An engine with a particularly interesting history was GWR No. 1384. This originated as Watlington & Princes Risborough Railway No. 2, a 2-4-0T built by Sharp, Stewart & Co. in February 1876 as their No. 2578. It was taken over by the GWR on 1st July, 1883 and renumbered 1384. In 1886 it was used on the construction of the Bodmin Road to Bodmin branch and then loaned to the Lambourn Valley Railway when it opened in April 1898. No. 1384 also worked on the Wrington Vale Light Railway and the Culm Valley line before being sold out of service in April 1911. It became Weston, Clevedon & Portishead Light Railway No. 4 *Hesperus* and was cut up in June 1937.

The second half of the 1920s saw more locomotives visiting the CVLR as No. 1298 had been withdrawn in October 1926 and a replacement was required when No. 1300 required maintenance. GWR Nos. 1192 and 1196 fulfilled this role. No. 1192 was Sharp, Stewart & Co. No. 1681, ex-Cambrian Railways No. 57 *Maglona*, built in May 1866. Maglona was a Roman camp at Machynlleth. No. 1192 was Great Westernised in July 1923, sent to Exeter in 1927 and withdrawn from there in August 1929. Sister engine No. 1196, ex-No. 58 *Gladys* (Sharp, Stewart No. 1682) also built May 1866, was Great Westernised in April 1924. It was sent to Exeter from about July 1927 until December 1928 and also spent time working the CVLR before returning to Oswestry until withdrawal in April 1948. *Gladys* was named after the daughter of Earl Vane, Chairman of the Newtown & Machynlleth Railway.

The final unusual engine was 2-4-0T No. 1308 *Lady Margaret*. Built by Andrew Barclay & Co., works No. 156 in 1902 at a cost of £1,570, for the Liskeard & Looe Railway, she was acquired when the GWR took over working on 1st January, 1909. The GWR rebuilt No. 1308 in May 1929 after which she was shedded at Exeter to work the CVLR for a period, before being transferred to Oswestry where she remained until withdrawal in May 1948. *Lady Margaret* was named after the wife of Captain Spicer who had financed the connection to Liskeard, which opened in May 1901.

In 1932 Charles B. Collett produced a modern 0-4-2T. Weight on the leading coupled wheels was 13 tons 10 cwt and on the driving coupled and trailing wheels was 13 tons 18 cwt each. Numbered in the '48XX' series, when these numbers were required in 1946 for 2-8-0s converted to oil-burning, the 0-4-2Ts were renumbered in the '14XX' series. This class, together with the occasional use of non-auto fitted, but otherwise identical, '58XX' class, worked the branch until the end of steam as no other class was permitted. They were allowed to take 140 tons up the gradient to Hemyock and 180 tons returning to Tiverton Junction, i.e. five loaded milk tank wagons and a coach, whereas the maximum for Nos. 1298 and 1300 was 90 tons and 100 tons respectively.

An interesting development could have occurred in the 1920s when the GWR considered electrifying lines west of Taunton, partly to reduce the expense of working over the severe gradients and also to obviate the long haulage of coal from Welsh mines. A report in June 1927 proposed either electrifying the Culm Valley branch or using petrol-engined railcars. Had this electrification scheme

No. D2141 (83B Taunton and Tiverton Junction) seen on 31st August, 1965, view towards Hemyock milk factory.
Michael Farr

Class '25' No. 7577 on 4th January, 1972 with one empty milk tank stopping at Uffculme after passing over the level crossing in order for the guard to board the cab after closing the gates.
Col M.H. Cobb

been carried out, it would have been done in four stages with the Culm Valley being the last line to be converted. Sub-stations would have been at Culmstock and Hemyock. A total of £550 was allocated, but never used, to reconstruct bridges to support 'Blue' locomotives with a maximum axle weight of 17.6 tons.

From 9th September, 1963 BR diesel-mechanical 0-6-0s (later termed class '03') with Gardner 8L3 204 bhp engines took over working, No. D2140 being used on the first day. Tiverton Junction shed lost its class '03' early in 1968 after the Culm Valley branch had been strengthened to allow type '2' locomotives to work. As these were based at Exeter, the Tiverton Junction signing-on point closed. North British type '2' (later class '22') B-B diesel-hydraulic locomotives weighed 68 tons, had a 17 ton axle load and 1,100 bhp engines.

On 14th December, 1970 Beyer, Peacock type '3' 'Hymek' (later class '35') No. D7056 of 86A Cardiff Canton, B-B diesel-hydraulic locomotive weighing 76 tons, worked the milk train and it is believed that this was the first appearance of the class on the branch. Others subsequently headed a train occasionally. In 1971 the still considerable traffic flows, milk from Hemyock and grain to Uffculme, were normally worked by a class '22', grain traffic being propelled from Tiverton Junction. For its final years, the line was worked by class '25' B-B diesel-electric 1,250 bhp locomotives weighing 76 tons, No. D7677 being in charge on 7th October, 1973 when the regular milk train conveyed Railway, Correspondence & Travel Society members in additional brake vans. Class '25' No. 25063 worked the last train on 31st October, 1975.

Earlier in the 20th century, it was not unknown for driver Adolphus Hawkins to stop between Uffculme and Culmstock to catch rabbits in purse nets of his own manufacture. Crews sometimes stopped by Yondercott Farm to purchase eggs and potatoes. If shunting was performed within the time allowed, at least one footplate crew used the spare moments to visit the nearby London Inn at Uffculme. If they were likely to overstay their time, the station master recalled them by tooting the engine whistle. Imitating American Indians, some children applied their ear to a rail to ascertain the proximity of a train, or placed a ha'penny on a rail to get it expanded to penny-size. To discourage children from such dangerous practices, some fireman sprayed them with hot water from the pet pipe.

Table of locomotives known to have worked the branch since 1933

'48XX'/'14XX' class
1405, 4806, 1420, 1421, 4827, 1429, 1435, 1440, 1449, 1450, 1451, 1462, 1466, 1468, 1469, 1470, 1471

'58XX' class
5812*

Class '03'
D2119†, D2140, D2141†

Class '31'
D5530

Class '22'
D6330

Class '35'
D7056

Class '25'
25063, 25082, 25094, 25152 (as D7502), 25156 (D7506), 25215, 25227 (D7577), 25253, 25306 (D7656), 25326 (D7676), 25327 (D7677)

* Worked the branch for several years from when it was new.
† D2119 and D2141 later had their cabs cut down and were used for working the Burry Port & Gwendreath Valley Railway line.

THE CULM VALLEY LIGHT RAILWAY

The up milk train arriving at Uffculme on 21st October, 1973 behind class '31' No. 5530. Sacks of Spiller's cattle feed are in the foreground. *Col M.H. Cobb*

Class '25' No. 7577 in Crossways cutting with the bridge carrying the A38 road in the background, 4th January, 1972. *Col M.H. Cobb*

LOCOMOTIVES

Engine Sheds

The single track timber-built engine shed at Hemyock measured 55 ft by 18 ft and had a slate roof. It probably opened in October 1876. Immediately outside was a stone-built coal stage measuring 18 ft by 10 ft 6 in. and a pillar water tank fed from a reservoir situated in the garden of the farm north of the station, the pipe continuing across Millhayes Bridge to supply a farm on the south side of the River Culm. Hemyock shed closed on 21st October, 1929 after which the branch was worked from Tiverton Junction shed placed in the apex between the Tiverton branch and the up main line.

Tiverton Junction shed probably dated from 1848. It consisted of a single-road ex-broad gauge brick building, 45 ft by 19 ft with a slate roof and raised ventilator. Inside the shed was a 45 ft-long inspection pit and another pit, 46 ft in length, was immediately outside. Also outside the shed was a 34 ft 6 in. diameter turntable installed in 1895 and removed in May 1908. Locomotives usually worked facing Hemyock. The 26 ft by 13 ft coal stage stood to the east of the shed.

A tank on the down side supplied water cranes on the platforms, 'not drinking water' to the station and to the cattle pens. The tank was replenished by a petrol/paraffin pump housed on the up side. When water in the tank was low, a porter was sent to start the pump. Initially it used petrol, but when warmed up was changed to cheaper paraffin. This petrol/paraffin pump replaced a steam pump in November 1928 and in 1945 was itself superseded by an electric pump.

Quadrupling the main line necessitated moving the shed to slightly north of its original site. The new single-road shed, 65 ft by 20 ft, consisted of a steel frame with brick panel walls. For ventilation, the corrugated iron roof had a raised ridge. A small office and stores was built into the north-west corner. The coal stage immediately to the east was roofed. Opened in 1932, the shed closed on 5th October, 1964.

At Hemyock the early turn fireman booked on before his driver in order to raise steam, while the late turn fireman stayed on as he was responsible for the engine's disposal. In order to balance the hours of drivers and firemen, a midday train was operated with two drivers, one of whom carried out the firing duties.

Hemyock Locomotive Allocations

Date	Engine	Date	Engine
January 1901	1300	July-December 1920	1300
January-February 1920	1298	January 1921	1298
March 1920	1300	May 1922	1300
April 1920	1298	May 1929	1300
May 1920	1300	August 1929	1192
June 1920	1298		

Tiverton Junction Locomotive Allocations

Date	Engines	Date	Engines
1st January, 1934	4808, 5812	31st December, 1947	1435, 1449

Ex-Cambrian Railways No. 58 *Gladys* as GWR No. 1196 heads a down train at Uffculme c.1927. The coach is an ex-Manchester & Milford Railway vehicle. Notice the goods shed, *left*, which was removed in 1932, and the water tank, *right*. The headcode is surprising. *Lens of Sutton*

An up train leaves Culmstock c.1947. Coach No. 2312 is in brown wartime livery. On the left is the renewed cattle pen and its concrete apron to enable water used for washing-out the pen to drain away rather than sink into the ballast. *M.E.J. Deane courtesy Ian Bennett*

Chapter Eight

Coaches and Other Rolling Stock

The first coaches used on the CVLR were small three- and four-compartment stock. Shortly after opening, one of the coaches was ex-Monmouthshire Railway & Canal Co. (MR&C) GWR No. 1184, with 'Culm Valley' branded on its solebar. It was built by Smith & Willey, Liverpool in 1848. The MR&C was nominally let to the GWR on 1st August, 1875 before it eventually amalgamated with the GWR on 1st August, 1880. This 13 ft-long coach had small windows and one oil lamp economically lighting all three compartments as the divisions were only seat-back in height. The coach weighed five tons and was fitted with Mansell-type wheels. The door handles were below the waist, a feature customary with early coaches.

On 1st July, 1906 the Manchester & Milford Railway (M&MR) was leased to the GWR and shortly afterwards three of the coaches from this line were drafted to the Culm Valley to replace the elderly four-wheeled stock. Two of these M&MR vehicles, re-numbered by the GWR Nos. 7898 and 7899, had been built in 1895 as tri-composites, but the GWR modified them for the Culm Valley line by converting two compartments for guard/luggage use, leaving two first class and three third class compartments. As the coaches had short wheelbase bogies and the bodies, only about 41 ft in length, they were ideal for the branch. From 21st September, 1927 the Culm Valley passenger trains became third class-only, so these coaches became brake thirds and were renumbered 657 and 606. The third ex-M&MR coach, also with short wheelbase bogies, was slightly older, having been constructed in 1892 and was about 37 ft long. It was a brake third with three compartments and carried the GWR No. 3982. These coaches worked the branch until the 1930s when they were condemned: No. 3982 in 1930 and Nos. 606 and 657 in 1936 and 1938 respectively.

They were replaced by elderly GWR coaches Nos. 1963 and 1964. These had the same three-centre roofs as contemporary clerestories, but lacked glazing. They also had deeper panels over the windows. Built as Lot 836, Diagram D22, and completed on 12th June, 1897, they were brake thirds 51 ft by 8 ft 6¾ in. and used initially on the Tenby and Pembroke line. *Circa* 1945 clerestory five-compartment brake third No. 2312, a 50 ft by 8 ft 6¾ in. vehicle, Lot 972, Diagram D37, of 29th June, 1901 ran on the branch.

Early in 1950 the tradition of using Welsh coaches continued when Nos. 1963 and 1964 were replaced by two ex-Barry Railway coaches of 1920, Nos. W263W and W268W. They were 54 ft 6 in. by 8 ft 9 in. and tared at 26 tons. Although originally electrically lit, they were converted to gas lighting at Swindon because speed on the Culm Valley line was insufficient for the axle-driven dynamos to keep the batteries charged. They proved to be the very last gas-lit coaches on British Railways. Due to the economy effected by closing the BR gasworks at Exeter in 1962, rather than re-convert them to electric lighting, other vehicles were considered. Ex-Highworth branch brake second No. 1239, 57 ft by 8 ft 11 in. built on 4th February, 1939, which had its ventilators set well

View west from the goods shed platform at Hemyock c.1950. An 0-4-2T has run round the ex-Barry Railway coach and SR PMV.
M.E.J. Deane courtesy Ian Bennett

Ex-Barry Railway coach No. W268 at Hemyock c.1950 in 'blood and custard' livery. Note 'Culm Valley' on the end and the '26' which indicates its weight in tons. 'Culm Valley' is also branded on the sole bar. Built in 1920 the coach was 54 ft 6 in. in length. The gas tank can be seen below the centre of the coach and nearby is a locomotive ash heap. To the right is a pile of hay or straw - probably the sweepings from a horse box or cattle truck. A milk tank stands on the right.
B.L. Jackson

COACHES AND OTHER ROLLING STOCK 115

'14XX' class 0-4-2T No. 1421 at Tiverton Junction working the 1.42 pm to Hemyock on 8th June, 1961 with an ex-Eastern Region coach.   *Author*

Ex-Eastern Region coaches Nos. W87245E and W87270E at Tiverton Junction *c.*1963. The first letter indicates the Region using the coach and the last letter the Region where it originated.
Michael Farr

No. D2175 leaves Uffculme with a down train, 9th May, 1967. It has three Regent fuel tanks and two open wagons. The brake van is unfitted, but has a through vacuum pipe. Notice the shunting pole on the outside platform. On the far right can be seen one of the steps leading up to a bridge girder which doubles as a lineside path due to limited clearance at track level.
A.E West/South Western Circle

A milk tank at Hemyock, 21st September, 1959. *Michael Farr*

No. D2141 shunting at Uffculme, 31st August, 1965. The 20 ton grain wagon is No. 885411.
Michael Farr

Ex-LMS grain wagon No. M298659, built Derby 1934, Diagram 1689, Lot 755, in George Small's siding, 9th May, 1967. The tarpaulin indicates a leaking roof. The three-arc roof blends neatly with the sides. There are two sliding doors in the roof for loading and a bottom opening, 1 ft 3 in. square controlled by a handwheel on one side only, for discharge. Trap doors on each side are for maintenance. Ladders at each end, diagonally opposite, give access to the top hatches. Two small inspection windows are provided at the top of each end.   *A.E. West/South Western Circle*

down on the roof to conform to the loading gauge was a possibility, but in the event, two ex-LNER brake second coaches were used from the winter of 1962-63. The battery charging problem was solved by connecting them at Tiverton Junction overnight with a battery charger. Periodically they were worked to Exeter for cleaning and inspection. They continued in use until the end of the passenger services on 7th September, 1963.

The GWR Rule Book of 1936 said that with the exception of the eight-wheel passenger coaches specially located to work over the branch, all other eight-wheel vehicles, and also six-wheel stock was prohibited and articulated sets of six coaches were banned.

When two coaches were used on mixed trains, passengers travelled in the front vehicle while the guard rode in the rear coach which acted as a brake van in addition to carrying parcels and luggage. If only one coach was used, as it was the brake van it was required at the rear, so passengers rode behind loose-coupled wagons. (Until the last few years of the branch when curves were slightly eased, a 'Toad', the standard GWR brake van, was not permitted.)

After 1929 when the locomotive shed at Hemyock was closed and the train service started from Tiverton Junction, the branch coaches were generally left overnight in the goods shed. If both were required for a train, one was coupled to the engine before it collected wagons from the goods yard loop, and then the train reversed into the goods shed to collect the second coach as a brake van.

204 hp diesel-mechanical 0-6-0 shunter No. D2141 at Tiverton Junction, 31st August, 1965 with a grain wagon for Uffculme. The fitted brake van No. W35962 is branded 'Taunton RU'.
Michael Farr

Chapter Nine

Passenger Train Services

The branch opened on 29th May, 1876 with five mixed trains each way taking 45 minutes for the trip of 7¼ miles. The fact that the first train started at Tiverton Junction, and the last ended there, was because Hemyock locomotive shed was not ready. With the shed's completion the train service was reorganized at the beginning of October 1876 so that the first up train left Hemyock at 5.50 am and the first down left Tiverton Junction at 7.15 am. The service at the end of the day was modified to make the last up train leave Hemyock at 5.30 pm and the last down left Tiverton Junction at 6.30 pm. In January 1877 there were five up mixed trains and six down.

In March 1878 Newton, the CVLR Secretary, complained to the GWR regarding the slow speed of trains. T.W. Walton, GWR divisional superintendent replied that 91 per cent of the trains were punctual; that goods traffic could be handled by passenger trains and that running a separate goods train would entail deleting a passenger train from the timetable in order to make a path for it.

Walton carried out an interesting census which proved that trains were not generally overcrowded.

Up			Down		
Dep. time	No. of pass. dep. Hemyock	No. of pass. arr. Tiverton Jn	Dep. time	No. of pass. dep. Tiverton Jn	No. of pass. arr. at Hemyock
8.30 am	5	20	9.30 am	6	5
10.30 am	4	16	12.50 pm	12	4
2.50 pm	5	10	4.25 pm	13	5
5.20 pm	3	7	6.30 pm	11	5
8.20 pm	3	5	9.25 pm	6	2

One gentleman remarked regarding the speed of the branch train: 'I wish I'd brought my fishing rod; I could have had a few casts in the Culm as we went along'.

Early in 1879 the first up and down services were deleted from the timetable so the Culm Valley Directors asked for them to be reinstated. Their wish was granted on 1st June, 1879, though in October the service was reduced to four each way.

In August 1887 four trains ran each way, the first leaving Hemyock at the relatively late hour of 8.30 am. Apart from the first train which took 55 minutes, they were allowed 45 minutes each way. Two in each direction were Government trains in accordance with the Regulation of Railways Act of 1844 which required all passenger railways to run at least one train daily on all lines, calling at all stations, at a fare not exceeding one penny a mile and with a minimum overall speed of 12 mph.

The service for January to April 1902 consisted of four trains each way:

Down trains: 9.15 am, mixed 65 minutes; 12.20 pm, mixed 50 minutes; 4.45 pm, passenger 32 minutes; 8.25 pm, passenger 32 minutes.

CULM VALLEY BRANCH.
Narrow Gauge.

Single Line worked by Train Staff. The Train Staff Stations are Tiverton Junction and Hemyock.

Section.	Form of Staff and Ticket.	Colour of Ticket.
Tiverton Junction and Hemyock.	Square.	Green.

TIVERTON JUNCTION TO HEMYOCK.
Down Trains.

Miles.	STATIONS.			1 Pass.	2 Pass.	3 Pass.	4 Pass.	5	6	7	8	9
				A.M.	P.M.	P.M.	P.M.					
	Tiverton Junction	dep.		9 25	12 30	4 25	7 35	....	....	....	....	....
2	Cold Harbour Siding	,,		C R	—	—	—	..	..	..	..	..
2¾	Uffculme	,,		9 49	12 50	4 44	7 54	....	....	....	....	....
5	Culmstock	,,		10 4	1 0	4 59	8 9	..	..	..	..	..
6¼	Whitehall Siding	,,		C R	—	—	—	....	....	....	....	....
7¼	Hemyock	arr.		10 20	1 15	5 10	8 20	....	....	....	....	....

HEMYOCK TO TIVERTON JUNCTION.
Up Trains.

Miles.	STATIONS.			1 Pass.	2 Pass.	3 Pass.	4 Pass.	5	6	7	8	9
				A.M.	A.M.	P.M.	P.M.					
	Hemyock	dep.		8 30	10 30	2 35	5 20	....	....	....	....	....
1	Whitehall Siding	,,		—	—	—	—	....	....	....	....	....
2¼	Culmstock	,,		8 46	10 46	2 51	5 36	..	..	..	..	..
4½	Uffculme	,,		9 1	11 1	3 6	5 51	....	....	....	....	....
5¼	Cold Harbour Siding	,,		—	C R	—	—	..	..	..	..	..
7¼	Tiverton Junction	arr.		9 15	11 15	3 20	6 5	....	....	....	....	....

Extract from the Regulations made by the Board of Trade for the working of the Culm Valley Light Railway.

"That the said Railway shall be worked between Tiverton Junction and Hemyock Station by one Engine in steam combined with the absolute Block Telegraph system; that the rate of speed of the Trains shall not exceed fifteen miles an hour on any part of the said Railway; and that the Locomotive Engines, Carriages and Vehicles used on the Railway shall not have a greater weight than eight tons upon the rails on any one pair of wheels."

Working timetable October 1886.

PASSENGER TRAIN SERVICES

Tickets: paper, *above*; card, *below*. Ticket for the aborted last special train, *bottom*.

Above. Edmondson's ticket date press from Hemyock. It was purchased by the CVLR for £2 10s. 0d.

No. 1449 at Hemyock c.1950 with its GWR number still on the buffer beam. Having the smokebox door handles at 'six o'clock' is unusual. The two ex-Barry Railway coaches are separated by two vans. On the left is the cattle dock, catch point and goods shed. On the right is the former refreshment room. An ash pile stands in the foreground. *B.L. Jackson*

The 1.40 pm Tiverton Junction to Hemyock formed of No. 1435 (83C, Exeter) hauling brake third No. W263W, pauses at Culmstock on 4th July, 1956. *Hugh Ballantyne*

PASSENGER TRAIN SERVICES

Working timetable 1923.

Up trains: 8.15 am, passenger 33 minutes; 10.40 am, mixed 50 minutes; 2.40 pm, mixed 47 minutes; 5.45 pm, passenger 33 minutes.

In the 1920s the coaches were well-filled with adults travelling to work at Exeter, Taunton, Tiverton and intermediate stations, plus children attending school at Tiverton. Sunday schools had special coaches attached to branch trains to be taken onwards to such places as Exmouth and Teignmouth. Long Sunday school trains caused trouble when returning on the bank out of Tiverton Junction and on at least one occasion had to set back to take a longer run.

The timetable for September 1928 showed the innovation of a late morning short-working return Tiverton Junction to Uffculme - the newly-installed loop allowing this. Down trains were at 8.45, 11.40 am (to Uffculme), 12.50, 4.30 and 7.00 pm. Up trains departed at 7.44, 10.25 am, 12.10 (from Uffculme), 2.45 and 5.40 pm.

B.K. Cooper in the *Railway Magazine* for June 1936 sums up the Culm Valley driver's attitude to the timetable. Someone living in a lineside cottage had the following conversation with a driver: 'When be going, Bill?', 'I be going d'rectly, George'. 'Wull, du'ee wait a minute then; I be coming with 'ee!'

Today when it is not unusual for people to fly on day trips to the Continent, it is hard to realise how immobile many people were in the past. B.K. Cooper wrote in the *Railway Magazine*, February 1936:

> Only recently, in the village of Culmstock, an inhabitant who was no ancient by the local standards of longevity, admitted to the writer that he had never been to Axminster - sixteen miles away - and disclaimed all knowledge of the locality with a haste which hinted at a low estimate of the civilising influences radiated from Waterloo.

By July 1938 there were four down trains (8.45am, 12.50, 4.30, 7.00 pm) taking respectively 57, 48, 39 and 39 minutes and five up (7.30, 10.30 am, 2.35, 5.50, 8.05 pm) taking 35, 37, 50 and the final two 38 minutes. Except on Saturdays, a late morning train (11.30) ran Tiverton Junction to Uffculme and return (dep. 12.10 pm), while Saturdays-only the 11.30 am train ran from Tiverton Junction to Culmstock and back (at 12.07 pm) plus there were a late evening return trip Tiverton Junction (at 9.10 pm) to Hemyock arriving back at Tiverton Junction 10.40 pm.

The Sunday service on the branch was only for milk. It took empty tanks to Hemyock in the morning and brought them back loaded in the afternoon.

WESTERN  REGION

HOLIDAY RUNABOUT TICKETS

ISSUED ON ANY DAY FROM
29th APRIL to 27th OCTOBER, 1956
Available for ONE WEEK from date of issue
PROVIDE
UNLIMITED TRAVEL IN HOLIDAY AREAS
CORNISH RIVIERA, GLORIOUS DEVON
and SMILING SOMERSET

THIRD CLASS FARES

Areas Nos. 1, 2, 3, 4, 5, 6, 7, 11, 13, 20 and 21	17s. 6d. each	Areas Nos. 3A, 4A and 20A	24s. 6d. each
		Area No. 6A	25s. 0d. each
Areas Nos. 1A & 2A	22s. 6d. each	Areas Nos. 7A and 13A	27s. 6d. each

Children under Three years of age, Free; Three and under Fourteen years of age, Half-fare.

DEVON.
Nos. 20 and 20A.

Tickets are also issued including trips on River Dart steamers at an additional charge of 7s. 0d. 3rd class.
(Area No. 20A)

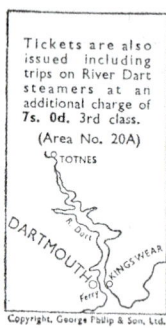
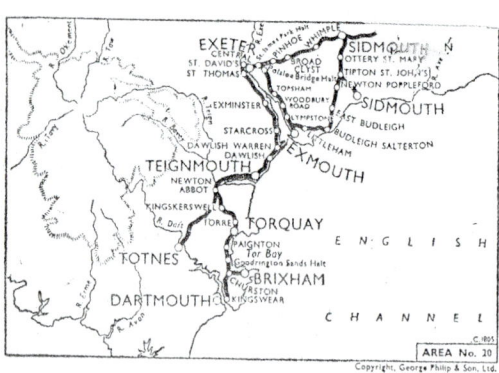

SOMERSET and DEVON.
No. 5.
17s. 6d.
3rd Class.

NOTE—Holiday Runabout Tickets are not available by the "Cornish Riviera" and "Torbay" Expresses during the period 11th June to 16th September inclusive.

Holiday Runabout ticket handbill, 1956.

General view of Hemyock station from the road bridge across the River Culm, 19th February, 1962. No. 1466 arrives, noted by the photographer to be 10 minutes early, with the 8.45 am from Tiverton Junction.
E.T. Gill

No. 1451 at Hemyock with coach No. W263. The River Culm runs between the meadow and the railway.
R.J. Sellick

An idyllic scene at Hemyock, No. 1470 and the reflection of the ex-Barry Railway coach in the River Culm.
Roger Holmes

'14XX' class 0-4-2T No. 1470 at Uffculme c.1955. Coal is stored in a fenced stacking area behind sleepers. Merchants were charged for space by the square yard. Anything above an agreed area was charged for, measurements being taken on a given date of the month.
Roger Holmes

PASSENGER TRAIN SERVICES

No. 1468 with the later BR crest and in lined green at Hemyock, 21st September, 1959.
Michael Farr

'14XX' class 0-4-2T No. 1421 at Uffculme with the 2.45 pm ex-Hemyock, 8th June, 1963. *Author*

'14XX' class 0-4-2T No. 1421 with the 5.10 pm Tiverton Junction to Hemyock between Tiverton Junction and Coldharbour Halt, 8th June, 1963. *Author*

No. 1421 at Hemyock with the 1.42 pm ex-Tiverton Junction, 8th June, 1963. The smokebox numberplate is missing from the brackets. *Author*

PASSENGER TRAIN SERVICES

No. 1421 approaches Whitehall Halt with the 2.45 pm ex-Hemyock, 8th June, 1963. Notice the steps up to the top of the bridge girder which doubles as a walkway. *Author*

By the summer of 1957 there were four down (8.45 am, 1.40, 4.30 and 7.05 pm) and five up trains (7.15, 10.30, 3.00, 5.55 and 7.52 pm) with a midday, Saturdays-excepted Tiverton Junction to Uffculme (11.25 am) and return (12.10 pm), while Saturdays-only it was extended to Culmstock and back (dep. 12.07). The fastest train was a Saturdays-only Tiverton Junction to Hemyock service (5.00 pm) taking 35 minutes, while the fastest up train took 37 minutes. On 15th September, 1958 the service was reduced to three down and four up trains, plus the short workings and this timetable continued until the end of passenger working. The odd working was balanced by an unadvertised run to Hemyock.

Table 85 TIVERTON JUNCTION and HEMYOCK
WEEK DAYS ONLY—(Second class only)

Miles		am E	am S	am S	am E	pm	pm	Miles		am S	am E	am	pm E	pm S	pm	pm
	Tiverton Junction .. dep	8 45	9 20	11 25	11 25	1 42	.. 5 10		Hemyock .. dep	7 10	7 15	10 30	..	..	2 45	6 0
2¼	Coldharbour Halt	8 55	9 30	11 35	11 35	1 52	.. 5 20	1	Whitehall Halt	7 15	7 20	10 35	..	..	2 50	6 5
2¾	Uffculme	8 58	9 33	11 39	11 39	1 55	.. 5 23	2¼	Culmstock Halt	7 22	7 27	10 43	..	12 9	2 59	6 13
5	Culmstock Halt	9 22	9 55	12 0	..	2 6	.. 5 34	4¼	Uffculme	7 33	7 38	10 54	12 20	12 20	3 11	6 24
6¾	Whitehall Halt	9 38	10 10	..	..	2 15	.. 5 43	5¼	Coldharbour Halt	7 36	7 41	10 57	12 25	12 25	3 16	6 28
7¾	Hemyock .... arr	9 43	10 16	..	..	2 20	.. 5 49	7¼	Tiverton Junction .. arr	7 47	7 52	11 10	12 38	12 38	3 27	6 39

E Except Saturdays   S Saturdays only

Last public timetable showing the passenger service, 17th June, 1963 to 8th September, 1963.

Culm Valley Branch.

Tiverton Junction to Hemyock. Note only the Special 8-wheel stock provided must work on this Branch—6-wheel stock prohibited.

Occupation of the Culm Valley Line between Tiverton Junction and Hemyock by Permanent Way Department.

1. The Engineering Department will have absolute occupation of the line between Tiverton Junction and Hemyock after the arrival of the last train at Hemyock until 15 minutes before the first train is due to leave Hemyock the following morning. If any work is taken in hand during that interval, and it cannot be completed 15 minutes before the first train is due to leave Hemyock the Ganger must act in accordance with Rule 251 of the Book of Rules and Regulations and also telephone to the nearest station in the direction from which the train is due. In such a case the train must be stopped and detained at that station until the Ganger advises the Station Master by telephone or otherwise that the line is clear.

2. No special train must be run during the time the Engineers have absolute occupation at night. (see Clause 1) unless written notice has been previously given to the Ganger, and his receipt is held for it.

3. To obviate the necessity for sending out Flagmen in accordance with Rule 251 of the Book of Rules and Regulations, when it is necessary to carry out operations (except as shown in Clause 1) which would render the running of trains unsafe, Telephones for use of the Ganger to communicate with either of the stations on the line are fixed in huts at the following points, and the instructions shown below must be strictly carried out :—

Places where Telephones are fixed, giving distance from Tiverton Junction.		Station to be telephoned to.	
Distance from Tiverton Junc.	Between.	For Up Trains.	For Down Trains.
Miles. Chains.			
60	Tiverton Junction and Uffculme.	Uffculme.	Tiverton Junc.
1 40	,, ,, ,,		
2 14	At Coldharbour Siding.		
3 50	Uffculme and Culmstock.	Culmstock.	Uffculme.
4 20	,, ,, ,,		
5 57	Culmstock and Hemyock.	Hemyock.	Culmstock.
6 34	At Whitehall Siding.		

NOTE.—Telephones are also provided at the following stations :—Tiverton Junction, Uffculme, Culmstock, Hemyock.

4. The Telephone Code Calls for the various Stations on the line are as follows :—

Tiverton Junction. Uffculme. Culmstock. Hemyock.
No. of Rings 2. 3. 4. 5.

5. When an absolute occupation is necessary, except as shown in Clause 1, the Ganger himself must go to the nearest Telephone Hut and get the attention of the nearest Station in the direction from which the next train is due, by ringing the Telephone in accordance with the Telephone Code.

6. When the Ganger has gained the attention of the nearest Station in the direction from which the next train is due to arrive, he must make his requirements perfectly clear to the Station Master by stating :

(a) Hut from which message is being sent, giving the distance from Tiverton Junction as shown in these instructions.

(b) Length of time occupation is required.

The Station Master must then inform the Ganger the length of time the line may be occupied, having regard to the actual running of the trains ; and in deciding the time, the Station Master must arrange for the occupation to cease 15 minutes before the train is due to leave Tiverton Junction or Hemyock, as the case may be.

7. If the authority cannot be given for the occupation, the Station Master must make it perfectly clear to the Ganger, and the latter must acknowledge the message which he receives by repeating it, so that there shall be a perfect understanding between the Station Master and Ganger.

8. If the Station Master can permit the work to be done, he must not under any circumstances, after having given such permission, allow a train to proceed past his station in the direction of where the occupation of the line is authorised, until he has received a message from the Ganger, clear and explicit, that the work has been completed and that the train may come forward. The Ganger must, on completion of the occupation, immediately advise the Station Master who has given the authority that the line is clear, and the Station must repeat the message to the Ganger to show that he understands it.

9. These instructions do not in any way relieve the Ganger from taking the necessary steps to protect the line in case of emergency, and when there is no time to communicate by Telephone to a station to stop a train ; but in such cases the Ganger is responsible for sending out a man in each direction with flags and detonators, in accordance with Rule 251 of the Book of Rules.

10. The time each Telephone message is received and sent with full particulars must be recorded by the Station Master concerned.

Appendix to No. 5 Section of the Service Time Tables (Exeter Division) May 1909.

Chapter Ten

Permanent Way and Signalling

Permanent Way

The initial permanent way consisted of flat-bottomed rail in lengths of 15, 17½ and 21 ft weighing 40 lb./yd, bolted and spiked to half-round sleepers of creosoted Baltic timber. Ballast, spread to about a foot in depth, consisted of sand and gravel from the pit at Craddock. The sharpest curves had a radius of 4¾ chains. At the time of construction a navvy commented: It 'twines like a ... snake in a fit!'

The GWR relaid the branch with second-hand bullhead 45 ft rail weighing about 85 lb./yd, but one length of flat-bottomed rail remained in a siding at Hemyock until the late 1950s. Sleepers used were those which had been 'cascaded' from main line use. Clearances from lineside features such as fences were narrow and it was possible to touch trees from a coach. The line followed the lie of the land and had sudden gradient changes. All level crossing gates were not much wider than a farm gate. In latter steam days they were opened by the fireman and closed by the guard, but this did not cause much delay as they were situated near platforms. In 1972 some of the bullhead rail was replaced with modern flat-bottomed rail.

A report of 5th September, 1975 said that, apart from two lengths of flat-bottomed track, lifting the branch would yield little serviceable rail, it was mostly old and in lengths of 45 ft, 39 ft and below. Rails on the very sharp curves suffered from severe side-cut and it was due to this side-cut that relatively short sections of track had to be relaid, rather than longer sections as on main lines.

The permanent way was maintained by a ganger and six platelayers based at Uffculme. The ganger rode on a velocipede with two wheels at the front and one at the rear. It was propelled by hands and feet in a rowing motion. The packers used a pump trolley, three at each end facing inwards.

Signalling

Being a light railway, signalling was fairly minimal. The agreement with the Board of Trade was that only one engine would be in steam between Tiverton Junction and Hemyock. Additionally the Board of Trade insisted on the branch being divided into block sections. These were: Tiverton Junction to Uffculme; Uffculme to Culmstock and Culmstock to Hemyock. The signalling was installed by the lesser known firm of O. & F.H. Varley, Highbury. In view of the speed restriction of 15 mph, the Board of Trade allowed distant signals to be dispensed with, but insisted in crossings being protected with home signals. Two arms were economically fixed to one post, and the two spectacles shared one lamp.

CULM VALLEY BRANCH.

The Branch is worked between Tiverton Junction and Hemyock Stations by means of one engine in steam carrying a staff.

The speed of trains must not exceed 15 M.P.H. on any part of the Branch.

Engines, coaches, and vehicles used must not have a greater weight than 13 tons 18 cwts. on any one pair of wheels, except that loaded 20-ton Grain Wagons may work over the Branch to the Private Siding at Uffculme.

Special eight-wheel passenger coaches are provided to work on the Branch. Ordinary eight-wheel stock for passenger use, vehicles over 60 feet in length and also six-wheel stock (with the exception of six-wheel milk tanks) are prohibited from working over the Branch.

All passenger stock specially authorised for working over the Branch prohibited from using :—

UFFCULME	Loading Bank Siding.
	Short Siding.
	Cattle Pens.
WHITEHALL	Siding.
CULMSTOCK	Cattle Pens.
	Back Siding.

The Branch is worked by engines of the 0-4-2 tank type. The engine is prohibited from using :—

UFFCULME	Loading Bank Siding.
WHITEHALL	Siding.
CULMSTOCK	Loading Bank—not to approach within 30 yards of dead end.

The G.W. Standard Load Gauge applies over the branch.

Working of Level Crossing Gates.

Whenever it is necessary for a special train not conveying passengers to be run over the Culm Valley Branch outside the scheduled hours of the Branch working, in addition to the trains enumerated in No. 5 Service Book, the Fireman of the train will be responsible for opening and the Guard for closing the Level Crossing gates at

COLD HARBOUR,
UFFCULME,
CULMSTOCK,
WHITEHALL.

Drivers to bring the train to a stand to permit this.

Shunting towards Culm Valley Branch Line. Tiverton Junction.

To protect shunting towards the Culm Valley Branch Line whilst a train is on the branch, a stop board is fixed at 0 miles 25½ chains, worded "All Up trains must stop dead here." Drivers are reminded that shunting may be taking place ahead of the Home Signal, and they must proceed cautiously from the stop board and be prepared to stop at the Home Signal.

Occupation of the Culm Valley Branch line must not take place after a train has left Uffculme for Tiverton Junction.

Advice of Running.

Stations and Halts, Tiverton Junction to Hemyock and vice versa, must advise by telephone the station or halt in advance the departure time of each train.

OCCUPATION BY ENGINEERING DEPARTMENT.

In order to avoid sending out Handsignalmen in accordance with Rules 215 and 217, when it is necessary to run trollies along the line, or to carry out operations which would render the running of trains unsafe, telephone boxes have been fixed at the places named below :—

Places where telephones are fixed.		Station to be telephoned.	
Distance from Tiverton Junction.	Between.	For Up Trains.	For Down Trains.
Miles. Chains.			
— 60	Tiverton Junction and Uffculme.	} Uffculme.	Tiverton Junction Signal Box.
1 40	Tiverton Junction and Uffculme.		
2 14	At Coldharbour Siding.		
3 50	Uffculme and Culmstock.	} Culmstock.	Uffculme.
4 20	Uffculme and Culmstock.		
5 57	Culmstock and Hemyock.	} Hemyock.	Culmstock.
6 34	At Whitehall Siding.		

It will only be possible for the Ganger or man in charge to obtain occupation under these instructions when the Branch is open. If occupation is required at any other time, Handsignalmen must be sent out in accordance with Rules 215 and 217.

When occupation is required, the Ganger must go to the nearest telephone hut and call the nearest station in the direction from which the next train is due or the Signalman at Tiverton Junction and make his requirements perfectly clear to the person in charge by informing him from what hut he is speaking and the length of time that occupation is required.

If permission can be given, the occupation must cease 15 minutes before a train is due to leave Tiverton Junction or Hemyock.

If permission has been granted, no train must be permitted in the direction where an occupation has been authorised until the Ganger has given an assurance that the work has been completed and the line is clear.

ES85

UFFCULME.
Propelling Empty Coaching Stock Trains between Uffculme and Tiverton Junction.

Whenever it is necessary for a Special Passenger train to run from Tiverton Junction to Uffculme, the empty train may be propelled as between Uffculme and Tiverton Junction on the return journey, provided the train does not exceed an engine and brake-third in which the Guard must ride and keep a sharp look-out, and be prepared to hand-signal to the Driver. When the Train Staff is handed to the Driver at Tiverton Junction, he must verbally be warned that on the return journey he is to regard the line as clear to the Home Signal only. The Station Master at Tiverton Junction must arrange to advise the Station Master at Uffculme, and the Crossing Keeper at Cold Harbour, when this working is being adopted.

HEMYOCK.

No vehicle must be allowed to remain at the dead end buffer stop.

Traffic to and from the Private Sidings is worked across the public road under the following instructions :

Siding protected by Level Crossing Gates.

The shunting is performed by G.W. engine.

Shunting with an engine across the public road must only be performed during the hours of daylight and at such times as the station work will permit.

The key of the Level Crossing gates is kept by the Occupiers of the Private Siding, and when wagons have to be taken across the public road they will arrange for the working of the gates and the provision of the Level Crossing. The gates must be kept padlocked except when it is necessary to shunt the Siding.

A wheel stop is fixed in the Cattle Pens Siding as a protection against the public road, and the key is kept by the person in charge of the station. The wheel stop must be kept padlocked across the rail except when the Private Siding is being shunted.

Care must be exercised to prevent wagons being pushed over the wheel stop.

Siding not protected by Level Crossing Gates.

Traffic is either propelled into or drawn from this Siding by means of additional wagons attached to the G.W. engine, and the engine must not pass over the public road.

Shunting across the public road must only be performed during the hours of daylight and at such times as the station work will permit.

The Occupiers of the Private Siding will be responsible for the protection of the Crossing.

Suitable warning boards are fixed on either side of the Crossing.

A wheel stop is fixed in the Goods Yard Siding as a protection against the public road and the key kept by the person in charge of the station. The wheel stop must be kept padlocked across the rail except when the Private Siding is being shunted.

Appendix to No. 5 Section of the Service Time Table February 1947.

PERMANENT WAY AND SIGNALLING

A guard closes Culmstock level crossing gates after a train has passed, 31st August, 1965.
Michael Farr

Milepost 1, 20th September, 1974, cast completely of iron. Note the check rail and spring metal keys.
Col M.H. Cobb

A permanent way train collecting rails and hauled by No. 25253, approaches the crossing point of the M5 motorway under construction, 28th October, 1975. *Col M.H. Cobb*

View 13th August, 1976 of the stub of the former Hemyock branch at Tiverton Junction used for storing a tamping machine. The M5 is in the background. To the machine's right is the 1 in 66 gradient post. To the right of the down loop, foreground, is concrete troughing in readiness for colour light signalling which was to supersede the semaphore signalling. *Col M.H. Cobb*

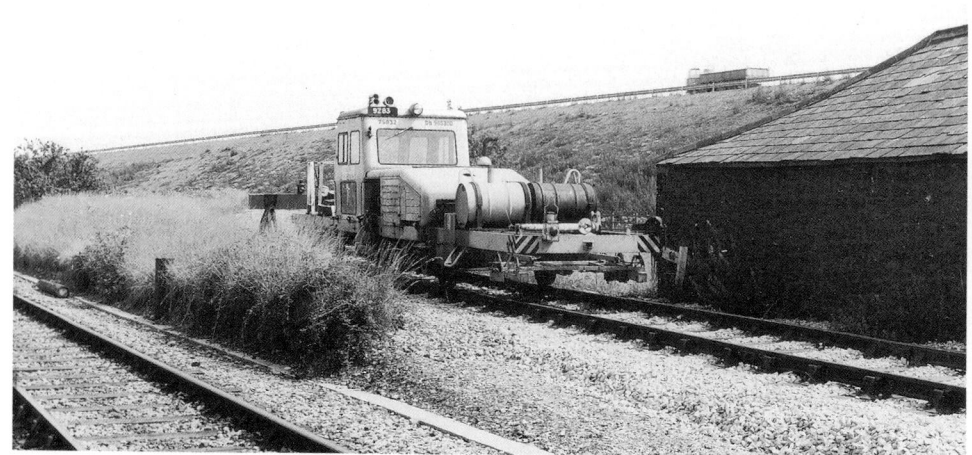

PERMANENT WAY AND SIGNALLING 135

In 1902 when the signalling system required renewal, the GWR drew the attention of the Board of Trade to the fact that the absolute block system under its Order of 23rd May, 1876 was superfluous when the line was worked by one engine in steam. The Board agreed and even said that the signals could be dispensed with. In return for being allowed to abolish the block system on the branch, on 15th May, 1902 the GWR made an undertaking:

> This railway shall be worked between Tiverton Junction and Hemyock Station by means of one Engine in steam carrying the staff; that the rate of speed of Trains shall not exceed fifteen miles an hour on any part of the said Railway; and the Locomotive Engines, Carriages and Vehicles used on the Railway shall not have a greater weight than eight tons upon the rails on any one pair of wheels.

It was probably at this time that the level crossings were protected on their western side by fixed distant signals. Those on the eastern side would have been superfluous as stations, apart from Coldharbour Halt, were to the east of the crossings. Fogmen were never used.

At Tiverton Junction the Culm Valley Branch signal box on the down platform controlled home, starting and shunting signals for the branch. It was reduced to a ground frame in the 1920s and taken out of use 31st July, 1932. Following the quadrupling though Tiverton Junction, the new main line signal box, opened on 25th September, 1932 on the up platform, controlled the branch signals.

Telephone circuit codes Tiverton to Hemyock.

Telephone circuit codes Tiverton Junction.

THE CULM VALLEY LIGHT RAILWAY

	Ground Frames and Intermediate Sidings—continued.		
Name of Station or Siding.	Where situated.	By whom attended.	How Locked.
		CULM VALLEY BRANCH.	
Uffculme	Private Siding	Station Master, Guard, or Porter	Key on Staff
,,	West end of Yard	Station Master, Guard, or Porter	,, ,, ,,
,,	East end of Yard	Station Master, Guard, or Porter	,, ,, ,,
Culmstock	Cold Harbour	Crossing Keeper or Guard	,, ,, ,,
,,	West end of Yard	Guard or Porter	,, ,, ,,
Hemyock	East end of Yard	Guard or Porter	,, ,, ,,
,,	Whitehall	Crossing Keeper or Guard	,, ,, ,,
,,	West end of Loop	Station Master, Guard, or Porter	,, ,, ,,
,,	On Platform	Station Master, Guard, or Porter	,, ,, ,,

Ground frames and intermediate sidings from the 1947 Appendix to the Working Timetable.

Culmstock cash bag.

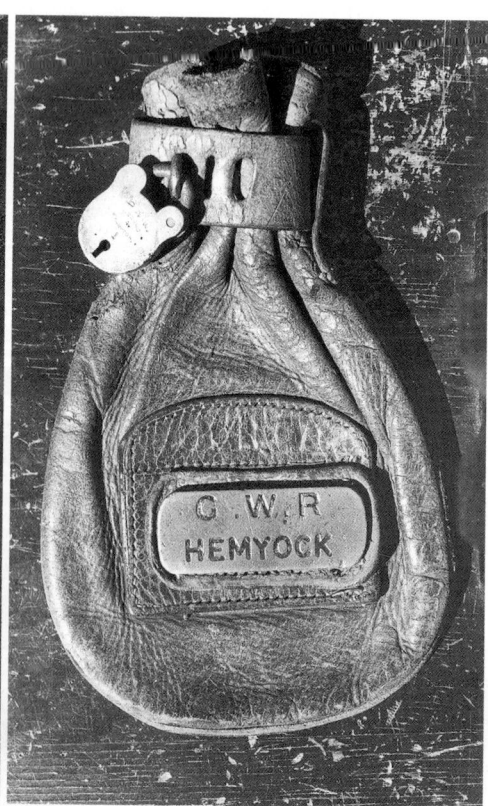

Hemyock cash bag. These were used for transferring station takings to the local accountant's office at Exeter.

PERMANENT WAY AND SIGNALLING

In 1931 the old telephone system dating from at least 1909 was renewed at a cost of £720. This installation permitted a new method of control whereby all stations and halts advised the next train's departure.

The *Appendix to the No. 5 Section of the Service Time Tables*, May 1909 stated that gatekeepers were at Coldharbour, Uffculme, Five Fords, Culmstock and Whitehall and that the working of sidings was:

Location	Person responsible for working the siding
Cold Harbour	Gatekeeper
Uffculme	Guard or porter
Culmstock	Guard or station master
Whitehall	Gatekeeper or guard
Hemyock	Guard or porter

The sidings were unlocked by Annett's key; a driver calling at a siding to be worked was required to hand the staff to the person appointed to be in attendance and was not to resume his journey until the staff was returned to him. The shape of the staff was square and the colour green. A station master was responsible for the exchange of the staff when on duty and the foreman, or ticket collector, when the station master was off duty.

From September 1964 a stop lamp was fixed at Tiverton Junction beside the up line, an engine and van length ahead of the handpoints leading to the goods shed line and all up Culm Valley trains were required to come to a stand at this lamp until instructed by a shunter to proceed.

Staffs: upper used in diesel days, ex-Penwithers Junction to Newham; lower, used from at least 1911 until the end of the passenger service.

Chapter Eleven

Mishaps

Mercifully the line was free from serious accident and even mishaps were few. A derailment occurred in July 1876, perhaps due to excessive speed, because soon after the line had been opened, Pain noted that speeds were 25 to 30 mph, rather than the 15 mph limit imposed by the Board of Trade.

On 3rd January, 1877, following very heavy rain, the railway embankment east of Uffculme formed a dam and, when the flood reached the top, washed away about 20 ft of ballast. The first train negotiated the hazard without derailing, but the jolt threw the fireman from the footplate into the water so traffic was wisely stopped. Repairs were carried out so rapidly that the evening train was able to run as usual. To prevent a reccurrence, a fortnight later Pain drove a culvert through the embankment.

The occasional farm animal trespassed on the line and got killed. An example of this was on 24th August, 1878 when the 8.20 pm Hemyock to Tiverton Junction killed a sheep half a mile before reaching Uffculme station.

On 21st August, 1879 the engine of the 9.25 am ex-Tiverton Junction, while shunting at Uffculme, came off the road and it took an hour to re-rail. Then at Whitehall Siding, guard Guppy, perhaps in haste to try and regain some of the lost time, while coupling wagons caught the forefinger of his left hand in the chain and squeezed the top of his finger off.

In 1927 a horse box was passed under the loading gauge and sent to Hemyock to collect a horse for transit to the Irish Republic via Fishguard. As it was getting dark the oil lamp for the groom's compartment was lit and placed in the hole in the roof, the lamp projecting about 9 in. When it passed under a bridge at Crossways cutting, it was smashed and fell, igniting hay and straw. The box arrived at Tiverton Junction belching smoke and flames. Fortunately the horse was released before it was seriously injured.

In early October 1960, following very heavy rain and subsequent flooding, the driver of the early morning train felt the track give way beneath him and his engine came to rest on the buffers of the leading coach.

Through the years, various breakdown cranes have been permitted to use the branch. In May 1909 the Exeter breakdown gang was used, while by March 1960 Newton Abbot 15 ton crane No. 8 was allowed, as was Bristol's 36 ton crane No. 1 and Swindon Chief Mechanical & Electrical Engineer's Department 45 ton crane No. 19, but Newton Abbot's 36 ton crane No. 3 and Swindon's 20 ton crane No. 5 were prohibited. In September 1969 45 ton crane No. 19, now at Bristol, Bath Road, was permitted on the the branch. In October 1973 Plymouth Laira 45 ton crane No. 151 was the authorized crane. The *Sectional Appendix to the Working Time Table for Exeter District* dated March 1960 gave instructions for emergency working:

> When in connection with an emergency it has been necessary for an engine or train to enter upon the Branch to render assistance and line or lines are again clear, the engine or engine of such a train may be coupled to the engine of the train which was disabled for the purpose of clearing the Branch Line or resuming the Service. In such circumstances the staff must be carried by the driver of the rearmost engine in the direction of travel.
>
> The working of such engines coupled together is subject to the restrictions shown in Section C of the Working Time Tables.

Appendix One

Bridges on the Culm Valley Branch

Bridge No.	Mileage from zero at Tiverton Jn M. C.	Local name	Function	Type	Remarks
1	0 02	Halberton	Railway over public road	Steel	Originally an arch; also carries main line.
2	0 23	-	Accommodation road over railway	Timber	3 spans
3	0 37½	Halberton	Public road over railway	Arch	A373
4	0 40	Willand	Public road over railway	Arch	A38
5	1 40	Southey Millstream	Level crossing approach over stream on up side	Steel	Originally 3-span timber bridge, reconstructed 1947.
6	1 40½	-	Railway over watercourse	Steel	Originally timber bridge, reconstructed 1939.
7	1 60½	Mill Stream	Railway over watercourse	Steel	Originally 6-span timber viaduct, reconstructed 1921 as one 80 ft span.
8	1 75½	-	Railway over watercourse	Concrete	Originally timber.
9	2 46	Mill Stream	Railway over watercourse	Steel	Originally 2-span timber bridge, reconstructed 1916 as single span.
10	2 64½	River Culm	Railway over watercourse	Steel	Originally 7-span timber viaduct, reconstructed 1918 as 2 spans.
11	2 71	-	Railway over watercourse	Barlow rails	Originally timber bridge, reconstructed 1916.
12	2 78½	-	Railway over watercourse		Timber bridge, replaced 1932 by concrete pipes.
13	3 57½	-	Railway over watercourse	Concrete	Orignally timber bridge, reconstructed 1934.
14	3 63	Craddock Stream	Railway over watercourse	Steel	Originally 2-span timber bridge, reconstructed 1920 as single span.
15	4 15	Southey Farm Road	Level crossing approach over River Culm on down side	Timber	3 spans
-	4 15	-	Level crossing approach over watercourse on up side	Arch	
16	4 21	-	Railway over watercourse	Barlow Rails	Originally timber bridge, reconstructed 1914.

Bridge No.	Mileage from zero at Tiverton Jn M. C.	Local name	Function	Type	Remarks
17	4 28½	Southey	Railway over watercourse (River Culm)	Steel	Originally an 8-span timber viaduct, reconstructed 1919 as 3 spans.
18	4 31	-	Railway over watercourse		Timber bridge, replaced 1932 by concrete pipes.
19	4 41	-	Railway over watercourse	Steel?	Originally timber bridge, reconstructed 1922.
20	5 00	Millstream	Railway over watercourse	Timber	2 spans. Replaced in 1944 by concrete pipes.
21	5 00	Millstream	Siding over watercourse	Timber	2 spans. Replaced in 1944 by concrete pipes.
-	5 00	Millstream	Siding over watercourse	Timber	2 spans. Replaced in 1944 by concrete pipes.
22	5 23	-	Railway over watercourse		Originally timber bridge, replaced 1915 by concrete pipes.
23	5 39½	Millstream	Railway over watercourse		Originally 3-span timber bridge, reconstructed 1922 as a single span, then replaced 1944 by concrete pipes.
24	5 46	Pook's Millstream	Level crossing approach over watercourse on up side	Timber	
25	6 24	-	Plank footbridge over stream on up side	Timber	
26	6 34	Millstream	Railway over watercourse	Timber	Originally 3-span timber bridge, reconstructed 1944 as a single span using material from bridge at 5 m. 39½ c.
27	6 36	Millstream	Railway over watercourse	Steel	Originally 3-span timber bridge, reconstructed 1921 as a single span.
28	6 46	Millstream	Railway over watercourse	Steel	Originally 5-span timber viaduct, reconstructed 1921 as a single span.
29	6 62½	Millstream	Railway over watercourse	Concrete	Originally timber, reconstructed 1947.

Appendix Two

Log of Journey
Tiverton Junction to Hemyock
on 8th June, 1963

Engine: '14XX' class 0-4-2T No. 1421
Coaches: 1
Average speed: 19 mph

Time m.s.	Distance	Station	Scheduled arr.	Actual arr. h.m.s.	Scheduled dep.	Actual dep. h.m.s.
–	–	Tiverton Junction	–	–	1.42	1.51.20
7.20	2¼	Coldharbour Halt	1.58.40	1.52	1.59.52	
2.11	2¾	Uffculme	2.02.03	1.56	2.03.38	
5.30	5	Culmstock Halt	2.09.08	2.06	2.12.35	
5.05	6½	Whitehall Halt	2.17.40	2.15	2.18.40	
3.20	7	Hemyock	2.20	2.22.00	–	–

Note
The train's departure time from Tiverton Junction was delayed as it had to await a connection.

No. 1421 arrives at Hemyock with the 1.42 pm ex-Tiverton Junction, 8th June, 1963.
Author

Bibliography

Books

The Tiverton Branch & The Hemyock Branch by C.H. Bastin (Author 1989).
Perlycross by R.D. Blackmore (Sampson Low, Marston & C, 1894; Three Rivers Books Ltd 1983).
Bradshaw's Railway Manual, Shareholders' Guide & Directory (various dates).
An Historical Survey of Selected Great Western Stations, Vol. 1 by R.H. Clark (OPC 1976).
Clinker's Register of Closed Passenger Stations & Goods Depots by C.R. Clinker (Avon-Anglia 1988).
Track Layout Diagrams of the GWR and BR/WR Section 15 by R.A. Cooke (Author 1986).
Great Western Coaches from 1890 by M. Harris (David & Charles 1985).
History of Willand Village by F.E. Janes (- 1969).
Great Western Branch Line Termini Vol. 2 by P. Karau (OPC 1978).
Light Railways Handbook by R.W. Kidner (Oakwood 1965).
History of the Great Western Railway Vol. 2 by E.T. MacDermot (Ian Allan 1964).
An Historical Survey of Great Western Engine Sheds 1947 by E. Lyons (OPC 1974).
Great Western Engine Sheds 1837-1947 by E. Lyons & E. Mountford (OPC 1979).
The Culm Valley Light Railway by M. Messenger (Twelveheads Press 1993).
Branch Lines Around Tiverton by V. Mitchell & K. Smith (Middleton Press 2001).
Locomotives of the Great Western Railway, various volumes (RCTS 1952 to 1993).
The Exe Valley Railway by J. Owen (Kingfisher 1985).
Great Western Railway Halts Vol. 1 by K. Robertson (Irwell 1990).
Great Western Railway Halts Vol. 2 by K. Robertson (KRB Publications 2002).
Uffculme, a Culm Valley Parish by Uffculme Local History Group (1988).
Great Western Branch Line Modelling, Parts 1 & 2, S. Williams (Wild Swan 1991).
The Culm Valley Light Railway by R. Crombleholme, D. Stuckey & C.F.D. Whetmath (Branch Line Handbooks 1964).

Magazine articles

'The Culm Valley Light Railway' Engineering, 16th October, 1874, p.300, Anon.
'Hemyock' Great Western Railway Journal No. 5, Winter 1993, p.202/3, Anon.
'Hemyock Branch' Railway Observer 1963, p.342-344, Anon.
'The Culm Valley Branch of the GWR' by B.K. Cooper, Railway Magazine, Vol. LXXVIII, p.116-120, p.423-426, 1936.
'Culm Valley - A Memoir' by B.K. Cooper, Railway World, Vol. 37, 1976, p.106-8, p.223, p.357
'The Culm Valley Light Railway by P.W. Gentry, Railway World, Vol. 14, 1953, p.38-40, p.119.
'Common Light Railway Architecture' by P. Karau, British Railway Journal, No. 1, 1983, p.25-31, No. 3, 1984, p. 60-63.
'Culm Valley Memories' by D. Lutley, Railway Magazine, 1987, p.176-178.
'The Culm Valley Branch' by R.C. Riley, Railway World, Vol. 23, 1962, p.369-372.
'Tiverton Junction' by C. Turner, Great Western Journal, No. 8, Autumn 1993, p.310-328.

BIBLIOGRAPHY

Acts of Parliament

36 Vict. cap. xxv The Culm Valley Light Railway Act 1873
37-8 Vict. cap. xxiii The Bristol & Exeter Railway Act 1874
38-9 Vict. cap. cxxvii The Bristol & Exeter Railway Act 1875

The National Archives, Kew

RAIL 147/1	Culm Valley Light Railway Directors' Minute Book
RAIL 147/10	Culm Valley Light Railway Traffic Returns
RAIL 253/158	Report on the Culm Valley branch.
RAIL 266/44	Great Western Railway Traffic Dealt with at Stations in the Exeter Division
RAIL1075/89	The Culm Valley Light Railway Prospectus
RAIL 1110/93	Culm Valley Light Railway Reports & Accounts
MT6/157/18	Board of Trade Report 22nd May, 1876
MT6/1079/1	Mode of Working

Newspapers

Bristol Times & Mirror
Devon & Somerset News
Tiverton Gazette
Tiverton Times

Acknowledgements

I would like to thank I. Bennett, Col M.H. Cobb, Amyas Crump, M.E.J. Deane, M. Farr, J. Gallop, J. Mann and the staff of Tiverton Museum for their valuable assistance.

Especial thanks are due to Colin Roberts for checking and improving the text.

Index

Figures in **BOLD** indicate illustrations.

Acts of Parliament, 5, 7 *et seq.*, 11, 15, 22, 36, 119
Bank of England, 9
Barnes, William, 19, 34, 36, 37
Barry Railway, 2, **63**, **72**, **79**, **85**, **88**, 113, **114**, **122**, **126**
Batten, John W., 35
Blackmore, R.D., 5
Blizzard, 39
Board of Trade, 19, 20, 21, 23, 25, 27, 28, 34, 37, 131, 135
Brereton R.P., 5
Bristol & Exeter Railway, 7, 9, 15, 17, 21, 22, 23, 25, 34, 36, 103
Broome, Richard, **16**, 17
Brunel, I.K., 5
Butter, 39, 43, 46, 47
Cambrian Railways, 107
Clements Bridge, 7
Clist, John, 39, 43
Coaches,
  Barry Railway, 2, **63**, **72**, **79**, **85**
  Great Western Railway, 3, 25, 27, 34
  Manchester & Milford Railway, **42**
  Other, 46, 66, 76, 85, 88, 92, 104, **106**, **112**, 113, **114**, **115**, 118, **122**, 123, 125
Coldharbour, 51, **54**, 55, **56**, **57**, 67, 87, 94, **128**, 135, 137, 141
Collett, C.B., 107
Commercial Inn, 8, 15
Contractors,
  Burt, Boston & Co., 11
  Crawshays, 11
  Hernelewicz & Co., 11
  Jardine, D.A., 11, 17
  Langdon, I.H., 11
  Patent Nut & Bolt Co., 11
  Sully, G.B., 11
  Varley, O.F. & C., 11
Coombes, George, 8
Cotton, William, 10
Craddock, 17, 20
Crossways Cutting, 17, 34, 51, **99**, **110**, 138
Culmbridge Mill, 8
Culm Davey Brick Co., 39, **40**, 67
Culm, River, 5, 7, 29, 31, **46**, 59, **88**, 90, 111, 119, **125**, **126**, 139
Culmstock, 5, 15, 17, 19, 20, 21, **22**, 23, 25, 29, 31, 34, 39, **41**, 43, 46, 55, 59, **64** *et seq.*, 67, **68**, 82, 83, **85**, 87, **101**, **112**, **122**, 123, 129, 131, **133**, **136**, 137, 141
Culm Valley Dairy Co., **42**, 43, 67, 81
Ellis, Henry Samuel, 8, 9, 15, 17, 19, 23, 26, 27, 31, 34
Farrant, Samuel, 39
Farrant, William, 7

Five Fords, 59, **63**, 137
Follett, Charles John, 8, 19, 34, 36, 39
Fox, Francis, 26
Fox, Messrs, 7, 29, 51, 55, 67
Fox, Walker, 17, 19, 107
Furze, William, 7, 8, 15, 19, 29, 34, 36, 37, **45**, 59
George Inn, 10
Godfrey's Railway Hotel, 15
Gradients, **24**, 51, 59, 67
Grain, **4**, 15, 109, **117**
Great Western Railway, 21, 22, 23, 25, 27, 28, 33, 34, 35, 36, 37, 39, **45**, 47, 55, 81, 107, 113, 118
Greenstone, 5
Grierson, James, 27, 28, 34
Hemyock, **1**, 3, 5, 7, 8 *et seq.*, 15, 17, 20 *et seq.*, 28, 29, **30**, 31, 34, 35, **38**, 39, 43, **44** *et seq.*, 51, 67, **72** *et seq.*, 81 *et seq.*, **88**, **90**, **92**, **94**, **95**, **97**, 101, **104**, **106**, 107, 109, 111, **114**, **116**, 118, 119, 121, **122**, 123, **125** *et seq.*, 129, 131, 135, **136**, 137, 141
Hemyock Stone & Coal Co., 43
Hind, Henry, 17, 19, 21, 22
Hutchinson, Major General, 51, 67
Ilminster Inn, 7
Lambourn Valley Railway, 107
Liskeard & Looe Railway, 107
Livestock, **45**, 47, 55, 59, **61**, 67, **79**, 83, 87, 101, 111, **112**
Locomotives,
  Diesel, **4**, **57**, **71**, 87, **93** *et seq.*, **108**, 109, **110**, **116** *et seq.*
  Henry Hind & Son, 17, 19, 21, 22
  Whitland & Taf Vale, **38**, 103
  Nos. 1192/1196, 107, 111, **112**
  Nos. 1298/1300, **38**, 103, **104**, **105**, 107, 111
  No. 1308, 107
  Nos. 1376/1377, 22, 23, 25, **102**, 103
  No. 1384, **42**, 107
  No. 1385, **102**
  '14XX'/'48XX' class, **1** *et seq.*, 54, 58, **61**, **63**, **66**, **68**, **69**, **72**, **74** *et seq.*, 78, **79**, 85, 87, **88** *et seq.*, **106**, 107, 111, **114**, **115**, **122**, **125** *et seq.*, 141
London & South Western Railway, 8, 35
Lutley, Edward, 8, 15, 22, 23, 39
Manchester & Milford Railway, **42**, **112**, 113
Milk, **1**, **3**, 43, 46, **57**, 83, 87, 94, **95** *et seq.*, 101, 107, 109, **110**
Millhayes, 7, 8, 43, 67, 111
Mishaps, 22, 138
National Provincial Bank, 8, 33 *et seq.*

New Inn, 8, 22
New, John Cave, 8
Newton, H. Cecil, 31, 34 *et seq.*, 119
Pain, Arthur, 5, 7, 9, 11, 15, 17, 18, 20, 22, 27, 34 *et seq.*, 55, 67, 138
Pearson, James, 103
Permanent way, 9, 11, 15, 17, 19, 20, 23, 25, 34, 35, 39, **42**, **45**, 59, **74**, 101, 131, **133**, **134**
Pollard, Frederick, 8, 19, 34
Porter, Henry Aylner, 8, 34, 36
Railway Inn, 31, 67, **68**
Selgar's Mills, 7, 8, 11, 27, 29, 51, **97**
Signalling, 11, 17, 20, 27, 28, **38**, 53, 55, 131, 134, 135, 137
Small, George, 45, 83, **85**, **89**, 93, 94, **117**
Southey, 7, 39, 139, 140
Star Hotel, 9, 31
Telegraph, 11, 17, 20, 27
Thomas, Henry Drew, 8
Timetables, 32, 40, 44, 56, 84, 86, 119 *et seq.*, 129, 132
Tiverton, 12, 23, 31
Tiverton & Devonshire Bank, 8, 15, 33
Tiverton Gazette, 7, 9, 20 *et seq.*, 28, 29, 32, 33, 39
Tiverton Junction, **2**, **4**, 7, 9, 11, 15, 17, 20, 23, 25, 27 *et seq.*, 31, 34, 39, 43, 47 *et seq.*, 51, **52**, **53**, 67, 87, **90** *et seq.*, 94, **96**, **98**, **99**, 107, 111, **115**, 119, **128**, 129, 131, 134, 135, 137, 138, 141
Tyrrell, George Nugent, 21
Uffculme, **4**, 5, 7, 8, 10, 15, 17, 19, 20, 21, 23, 27, 29, 31 *et seq.*, 38, 39, 43, **45**, 46, 47, 51, 55, 58, 59, **60** *et seq.*, 82, 83, **85**, 87, **89**, **93**, 94, 101, 109, **110**, **112**, **116** *et seq.*, 123, **127**, 129, 131, 137, 138, 141
Uffculme Brewery, 7
United Dairies, Wilts, 43, 46, **74**, 77, **79**, **80**, 81, 94
Wall, J.C., 9
Walrond, John, 15, 29, 34
Watlington & Princes Risborough Railway, 42, 107
Wellington Monument, 5, 21, 29
Weston, Clevedon & Portishead Light Railway, 107
Whitehall, 7, 8, 23, 55, 67, **69** *et seq.*, **100**, **129**, 137, 141
Wide, James, 39
Willand, 9
Woodhayne, 7
Wood, Misses, 8
Yates, James, 43
Yolland Col, 20, 21, 23, 25, 27, 28

144